Language in Education in Africa:
A Tanzanian Perspective

Multilingual Matters

Afrikaner Dissidents
  JOHA LOUW-POTGIETER
Bicultural and Trilingual Education
  MICHAEL BYRAM and JOHAN LEMAN (eds.)
Bilingual Children: From Birth to Teens
  GEORGE SAUNDERS
Bilingual and Multicultural Education: Canadian Perspectives
  S. SHAPSON and V. D'OYLEY (eds.)
Bilingualism in Society and School
  J. JØRGENSEN, E. HANSEN, A. HOLMEN and J. GIMBEL (eds.)
Cultural Studies in Foreign Language Education
  MICHAEL BYRAM
Current Trends in European Second Language Acquisition Research
  HANS W. DECHERT (ed.)
Dialect and Education: Some European Perspectives
  J. CHESHIRE, V. EDWARDS, H. MUNSTERMANN and B. WELTENS (eds.)
Every Child's Language
  (Open Univ Pack)
Key Issues in Bilingualism and Bilingual Education
  COLIN BAKER
Language Acquisition: The Age Factor
  D.M. SINGLETON
Language Attitudes Among Arabic-French Bilinguals in Morocco
  ABDELALI BENTAHILA
Language Distribution Issues in Bilingual Schooling
  R. JACOBSON and C. FALTIS (eds.)
Language in a Black Community
  VIV EDWARDS
Language and Education in Multilingual Settings
  BERNARD SPOLSKY (ed.)
Language Planning and Education in Australasia and the South Pacific
  R.B. BALDAUF and A. LUKE (eds.)
Minority Education: From Shame to Struggle
  T. SKUTNABB-KANGAS and J. CUMMINS (eds.)
Oral Language Across the Curriculum
  DAVID CORSON
Raising Children Bilingually: The Pre-School Years
  LENORE ARNBERG
The Role of the First Language in Second Language Learning
  HÅKAN RINGBOM
Schooling in a Plural Canada
  JOHN R. MALLEA
Second Language Acquisition — Foreign Language Learning
  B. VanPATTEN and J.F. LEE (eds.)
Story as Vehicle
  EDIE GARVIE
Variation in Second Language Acquisition (Vol. I and II)
  S. GASS, C. MADDEN, D. PRESTON and L. SELINKER (eds.)

Please contact us for the latest book information:
Multilingual Matters,
Bank House, 8a Hill Rd,
Clevedon, Avon BS21 7HH,
England

MULTILINGUAL MATTERS 57
Series Editor: Derrick Sharp

Language in Education in Africa: A Tanzanian Perspective

Edited by

Casmir M. Rubagumya

MULTILINGUAL MATTERS LTD
Clevedon · Philadelphia

Library of Congress Cataloging in Publication Data

Language in Education in Africa: Tanzanian Perspectives/edited by Casmir M.
Rubagumya
  (Multilingual Matters, 57).
  Bibliography. Includes Index.
  1. Native Language and Education – Tanzania. 2. English Language – Study
and Teaching – Tanzania. 3. Language Policy – Tanzania.
  I. Rubagumya, Casmir M. 1946– . II Series: Multilingual Matters, 57.
  LC201.7.T34L36   1989
  306.4'499678 – dc20

British Library Cataloguing in Publication Data

Language in Education in Africa: Tanzanian Perspectives (Multilingual Matters,
57).
  1. Tanzania. Schools. Teaching in English.
  I. Rubagumya, Casmir M.
  371.1'02

ISBN 1-85359-063-0
ISBN 1-85359-062-2 (pbk)

Multilingual Matters Ltd

Bank House, 8a Hill Road,   &   1900 Frost Road, Suite 101
Clevedon, Avon BS21 7HH,   Bristol, PA 19007
England   USA

Index compiled by Meg Davies (Society of Indexers).
Typeset by Morley Harris Typesetting, Bristol.
Printed and bound in Great Britain by WBC Print Ltd, Bristol.

Contents

Foreword
M. Martin-Jones vii

Acknowledgements ix

1. Introduction
   C.M. Rubagumya 1

2. Language in Tanzania
   C.M. Rubagumya 5

3. On the History of English Language Teaching in Tanzania:
   Three Theses
   A.F. Lwaitama, C.M. Rubagumya and M.K. Kapinga 15

4. Reflections on Recent Developments in Language Policy in
   Tanzania
   J.M. Rugemalira, C.M. Rubagumya, M.K. Kapinga,
   A.F. Lwaitama and J.G. Tetlow 25

5. The English Language Support Project in Tanzania
   A.F. Lwaitama and J.M. Rugemalira 36

6. When International Languages Clash: The Possible Detrimental
   Effects on Development of the Conflict between English and
   Kiswahili in Tanzania
   S. Yahya-Othman 42

7. English Language Teaching and Learning in Tanzanian Primary
   Schools
   H.M. Batibo 54

8. The Training of Secondary School Teachers of English in
   Tanzania
   Z.M. Roy-Campbell 75

9. Can a Foreign Language be a National Medium?
   H.R. Trappes-Lomax 94

10. The Communication Skills Unit and the Language Problem at
the University of Dar es Salaam
J.M. Rugemalira 105

11. Accepted Language Behaviour as a Basis for Language
Teaching: A Comparison of English in Kenya and Tanzania
J. Schmied 123

12. Swahili Terminological Modernisation in the Light of the
Present Language Policy of Tanzania
H. J.M. Mwansoko 133

13. Political and Economic Dimensions to Language Policy Options
in Tanzania
C.M. Rubagumya and A.F. Lwaitama 143

Index 153

Foreword

M. MARTIN-JONES

This book is an important new contribution to the literature on language in education in Africa. It is the first significant collection of articles on language policy issues in Tanzania to be edited by a Tanzanian linguist. Rubagumya has succeeded in putting together a most interesting and informative volume which reflects a coherent Tanzanian perspective on past and present policy developments.

The idea of a book on language in education in Tanzania grew out of a research seminar on bilingualism held at the University of Dar es Salaam in December, 1986. I was fortunate enough to be one of the participants in this seminar. In the course of our discussions, we became increasingly aware of the fact that little attention has so far been given to the views of Tanzanian linguists in both the academic and educational debates about language policy issues in Tanzania, particularly in the current controversy about the use of English as the medium of instruction in the secondary schools. At the end of the seminar several of the participants decided to write a joint paper outlining their analysis of recent developments in language education policy and making clear recommendations for future policy and practice. The paper was designed to have two functions: to serve as a discussion document in an interdisciplinary debate about language policy issues, which the authors hoped to initiate at the University of Dar es Salaam; and, secondly, to provide researchers outside the Tanzanian context with an update on recent policy developments from a specifically Tanzanian point of view.

This joint writing project soon led to plans for a book. It was felt that the joint paper should be published alongside other contributions from colleagues at the University of Dar es Salaam and from other researchers familiar with the Tanzanian context. In this way, the recommendations set out in the joint paper could be placed in a wider educational and historical context and the relationship between Kiswahili and English could be explored in greater detail. In his role as editor, Rubagumya has worked with enormous commitment, in very difficult circumstances, to ensure that this collection of articles reaches the wider audience it deserves. The outcome of these efforts is a major new publication of quality which will be widely read by those concerned with language policy in developing countries.

Lancaster, July 1988

Acknowledgements

This book is a concrete outcome of an academic link which exists between the Department of Foreign Languages and Linguistics of the University of Dar es Salaam, Tanzania, and the Department of Linguistics of Lancaster University, UK, under the auspices of the British Council. The preparation of the book was triggered by a series of seminars on Bilingualism held in Dar es Salaam in December 1986. These seminars were part of the activities of the link programme. I subsequently edited this volume when I was on study leave at Lancaster University in 1988, again as part of the link activities.

I am very grateful to Dr Marilyn Martin-Jones of the Department of Linguistics, Lancaster University, for her constant encouragement and support, and to the British Council for financial assistance in the preparation of the manuscript (word-processing and photocopying).

C.M. Rubagumya
Lancaster, July 1989

1 Introduction

C.M. RUBAGUMYA

Tanzania is often given as a shining example of successful language planning in favour of an indigenous African language. For example, Phillipson *et al.* (1986: 91) argue that there is a general shift in the direction of favouring European languages as media of instruction in African countries. They claim that 'Tanzania is an exception to this rule in sub-Saharan Africa, as is Somalia'. While it is true that Tanzania has made a lot of progress in cultivating Kiswahili as a viable national language which is now used in almost all spheres of national life, in the education field Tanzania's success is usually exaggerated by outsiders.

Tanzania, like most African countries, still considers the language of the former colonial rulers (in this case English) as the most suitable as a medium of instruction above the primary school level. However, unlike most African countries, the Tanzanian authorities have on several occasions declared their intention to change the medium of instruction from English to Kiswahili (see chapters by Trappes-Lomax and Yahya-Othman in this volume). The question is: why has Tanzania been unable or unwilling to change the medium of instruction as envisaged?

Fasold (1984: 292) argues that there are three main considerations in choosing a language of instruction:

1. do the prospective students know the language well enough to learn effectively through it?

2. would the proposed choice be consistent with overall nationalist aims?

3. are the language itself, the material written in it, and the number of people able to teach in it adequate for use at the proposed level?

Fasold goes on to claim that 'Swahili would be the choice for higher education in Tanzania on the first two criteria, but is prevented on the third one'. But, as is made clear in several chapters in this volume, neither the materials written in English nor the people capable of teaching in it are adequate in Tanzania today. So, clearly, Fasold's third criterion cannot be the only reason, nor even the main one, why Kiswahili is not the medium of instruction in secondary and higher education.

The main reason, I would venture to suggest, is that in Tanzania, again as in many other African countries, the former colonial language is seen as a prerequisite for scientific and technological development. Examples abound everywhere in Africa to underscore this. For example, in Nkrumah's Ghana English was deliberately given a high status over African languages because the Nkrumah regime believed English was the key to technological progress and modernity. Paradoxically, Nkrumah saw in English, the language of colonial domination, a tool for the total liberation and radical transformation of Ghana in particular, and Africa in general (Verlet, 1986). Recent policy pronouncements in Tanzania, discussed in this volume, have tended to show that the main objection to the use of Kiswahili as the medium of instruction is not so much because Kiswahili is inadequate for the purpose, but because, it is claimed, if English is not used as the medium, Tanzania will be 'left behind' with respect to scientific and technological development.

Another reason, which is rarely stated in public, has to do with the very élitist nature of education in Africa. Talking about Zaire, Ngalasso (1986: 15) aptly sums up how European languages in Africa maintain this élitism:

> French has, in Zaire as in other Francophone African countries, a mythical, mystical, even mystifying function: since it is a sign of being knowledgeable, it is a magic key to social prestige and power. Its use rarely corresponds to real need; it is usually used to show that one has reached a level of linguistic competence which entitles one to a legitimate claim to power, and eventually to mystify (those who don't speak the language). [My translation]

In most African countries, Tanzania included, English, French or Portuguese play the same role as that described above. This of course reinforces the belief that education is not possible without a European language, hence the scepticism of the general public when suggestions of changing the medium of instruction are made. Understandably, all parents would like their children to climb the 'ladder of success' to the highest level possible.

What is sometimes not appreciated is that the pursuit of this élitist education is in conflict with stated policies. Thus, in Tanzania it is difficult to see how 'Education for Self-Reliance' can be consistent with education which uses English as the medium of instruction. If education is meant to prepare the majority for the type of life they are likely to lead (i.e. in rural areas) rather than to favour only a few, it would seem that Kiswahili is better suited to that task. Talking about the inconsistency between the dominance of French language and the policy of 'authenticity' in Zaire, Ngalasso (1986: 25) comments:

> It should be stressed that in implementing the policy of authenticity, whether in schools, the economy or political institutions, there is hardly any in-depth analysis. Only superficial elements of authenticity such as folklore, dress, titles, are addressed. [My translation]

It hardly needs any comment that 'authenticity' cannot be brought about only by changing one's Christian name, by rejecting the Western suit (but not the Western values) and by changing someone's title from '*Monsieur*' to '*Citoyen*' (both terms are French anyway)! Likewise, Education for Self-Reliance cannot be achieved by attaching to the school a token '*shamba*' (farm, garden) while the whole system is still geared to the selection of a few who will 'make it' to the top.

The aim of this book is to attempt to paint a more realistic picture of the situation in Tanzania today concerning the statuses of Kiswahili and English. It is intended to make available to a wider audience insights into the present debate as to which language should be used as the medium of instruction, the problems of English language teaching in Tanzania, and the whole question of language in education generally. We hope that the Tanzanian experience will be of interest to all those in multilingual settings in general, and those interested in language and education in Africa in particular.

The chapters contained in this volume are varied in approach. While some of them question the foundation on which the present language policies in Africa — and in Tanzania in particular — are built, others attempt to suggest what can be done to minimise the existing problems of language in education, given the prevailing policies. There is no contradiction between the two approaches. The message of this volume is: there is need to change the present language policies in education in Africa. But, while we work towards that ultimate goal, some actions can be taken immediately to address the problems inherent in the prevailing policies. Individual contributors to this volume may not agree on the strategies to solve the problems discussed, but they all agree that these problems do exist and they share the same concern. They certainly do not claim to have provided the (only) answers to the issues raised. If this volume succeeds in stimulating more debate and research, and if it draws some attention of African decision makers to those issues, it will have achieved its purpose.

References

FASOLD, R. 1984, *The Sociolinguistics of Society*. Oxford: Basil Blackwell.
NGALASSO, M.M. 1986, Etats des langues et langues de l'état au Zaire. *Politique Africaine*, no. 23.
PHILLIPSON, R., SKUTNABB-KANGAS, T. and AFRICA, H. 1986, Namibian educational language planning: English for liberation or neo-colonialism? In B. SPOLSKY (ed.) *Language and Education in Multilingual Settings*. Clevedon: Multilingual Matters.
VERLET, M. 1986, Les maîtres-mots: langue et pouvoir au Ghana sous Nkrumah. *Politique Africaine*, no. 23.

2 Language in Tanzania

C.M. RUBAGUMYA

Kiswahili vs. English: An Historical Overview

Some form of proto-standard Kiswahili was being spoken on the coast of East Africa before the tenth century (Whiteley, 1969). However, it was not until the nineteenth century that the language started to spread into the interior of East and Central Africa. According to Whiteley (1969) the expansion of Kiswahili inland from the coast falls into two phases:

> In the first, from about 1800 to 1850, the country was gradually opened up by trading caravans, who took the language with them in the form of a Swahili-speaking 'managerial' core; during the second phase, from around 1850 until the advent of the colonial powers, the first systematic studies of the language were made and used as a basis for teaching others. (p. 42)

Because the initial spread of Kiswahili into the interior of East Africa owes much to trade (in ivory, slaves, etc.) the pattern of trade in the nineteenth century partly explains why the language spread more quickly in Tanzania than in Kenya and Uganda, her northern neighbours. Commenting on the spread of Kiswahili, Mazrui & Zirimu (1978) argue:

> There were obstacles to internal trade which in turn served as obstacles to the further spread of Kiswahili. In some parts of Eastern Africa militantly protective communities acquired the reputation of ruthless hostility to foreigners, and were thus able to keep away many an enterprising merchant from the coast. The Masai in both Kenya and Tanganyika acquired this martial reputation, and therefore served as a hindrance to both the expansion of trade and the spread of Kiswahili, especially in Kenya. (p. 428)

When the Germans colonised part of East Africa (present-day Tanzania, Rwanda and Burundi) they found that Kiswahili was already fairly widespread. As they relied very heavily on Kiswahili-speaking coastal

5

people for the administration of the colony, this encouraged the spread of
the language even farther into the interior. The Germans promoted
Kiswahili on a large scale because it afforded considerable administrative
convenience. The impact of the period of German rule in Tanzania upon the
fortunes of the language in the country was considerable (Mazrui & Zirimu,
1978). During this period (1885–1919) Kiswahili was the medium of
instruction throughout the school system in the colony. German was taught
as a subject, but there was no real effort to promote it or to make it replace
Kiswahili as the medium of instruction. Also, administrative correspondence was carried out in Kiswahili (Cameron & Dodd, 1970). Because
Kiswahili was the language of administration,

> great efforts were made to document it, and scholars like Velten,
> Seidel, Buttner and others provided the materials on which courses at
> the Oriental Seminar in Berlin were based. A governor like
> Rechenberg (1906–1912) spoke the language, and his successor,
> H. Schnee, had attended courses in Berlin. (Whiteley, 1969: 59)

In contrast, in Uganda and Kenya Christian missionaries were opposed
to the use of Kiswahili in schools. The missionary hostility to the language is
here expressed in the words of Bishop Tucker of Uganda:

> That there should be one language for Central Africa is a consumma-
> tion devoutly to be wished, but God forbid that it should be Swahili.
> English? Yes! But Swahili never. The one means the Bible and
> Protestant Christianity, the other Mohammedanism . . . sensuality,
> moral and physical degradation and ruin . . . [Swahili is too closely
> related to Mohammedanism] to be welcome in any mission field in
> Central Africa. (Quoted in Mazrui & Zirimu, 1978: 431)

Presumably, the Bishop believed that all English speakers were
Bible-reading Protestant Christians, and moral; while all Kiswahili speakers
were Muslims, sensuous, morally and physically degraded and ruined. To
be saved, the trick was to learn English!

The same opposition to Kiswahili was expressed by the Kabaka (King)
of Buganda, Sir Daudi Chwa, in 1929, although his reasons were different
from those advanced by Bishop Tucker.

> . . . it is quite unnecessary to adopt the Kiswahili language as the
> official native language in Buganda, and I am entirely opposed to any
> arrangements which would in any way facilitate the ultimate adoption
> of this language as the official native language of the Baganda in place
> of, or at the expense of, their own language. (Quoted in Whiteley,
> 1969: 70)

When the British took over from the Germans at the end of World War I they maintained Kiswahili as a medium of instruction in the first five years of primary school. English was offered as a subject from the third year of primary school, and it replaced Kiswahili as the medium of instruction in the last three years of primary school. The secondary school medium of instruction was English, but Kiswahili was offered as a subject up to school certificate 'O' level.

Despite the hostility to Kiswahili by Christian missionaries and the Kabaka of Buganda, the governors of Kenya, Uganda, Tanganyika and Zanzibar were convinced that the language was a viable *lingua franca* for the whole of East Africa, and saw the need for its standardisation. With the approval of the Secretary of State for Colonies in London, the Inter-territorial (Swahili) Language Committee came into being on 1st January 1930 with the main aim of promoting the standardisation and development of Kiswahili. Some of its specific objectives were:

i. Standardising orthography and obtaining complete inter-territorial agreement.
ii. Securing as far as possible uniformity in the use of existing and new words by the exercise of control over publication of school and other dictionaries.
iii. Securing uniformity of grammar and syntax throughout the publication of standard books on the subject.
iv. Giving encouragement and assistance to authors whose native tongue is Swahili.
v. Making arrangements for translating into Swahili the textbooks and books of a general nature selected, or for direct authorship in Swahili of such books.
vi. Examining and, where necessary, correcting the Swahili of such textbooks and general literature before publication.

(Whiteley, 1969: 82–3)

However, the opposition to Kiswahili, even in Tanganyika, was not yet over. In 1953 the Binns Mission Report tried to persuade the colonial government in Tanganyika to get rid of Kiswahili in schools, on the grounds that its use was not in the interests of African children:

If a distinctive African contribution is to be made to the world it must be based on the African's love and respect for the mental inheritance of his people and much of this is enshrined in [the vernacular] language . . . The existence of Swahili . . . in Tanganyika and its place in school teaching is unfortunate for it seems to have affected adversely the teaching of *both the vernacular and English* . . . We suggest therefore that because *the present teaching of Swahili stands in the way of the strong development of both the vernacular and English teaching* a policy should be followed which leads to its eventual elimination from schools where it is taught as a *lingua franca*. (Quoted in Cameron & Dodd, 1970. My emphasis)

It is interesting to note that the position of English in the educational system was taken for granted. That is, the report did not question the possible effects of English on the children's mentality. To be fair to the Binns Mission, it would probably be unreasonable to expect the colonial government at that time to have provided education without the use of English. I am not questioning the sincerity of the Binns Mission. Most probably they put forward this proposal in good faith for what they believed to be in the best interest of African children: to give them education in a world language while at the same time they retain their cultural 'roots' through the vernacular. It would, however, have been quite difficult for the colonial government to implement this proposal. Getting rid of Kiswahili would have meant starting from scratch to standardise more than 120 vernaculars spoken in Tanzania. It was probably for this reason that the government rejected the proposal. Kiswahili therefore continued to be used in schools as well as in local administration.

It is worth noting here that the Binns Mission probably exaggerated the 'foreign' nature of Kiswahili to Tanzanian children. Experience has shown that Tanzanian children find it easier to learn Kiswahili than European languages like English. This is partly because they have a wider exposure to Kiswahili, and partly because most children speak a Bantu language as their mother tongue and therefore find it relatively easy to learn Kiswahili, which is also a Bantu language. In this respect, it seems to me that Moumouni (1967) is convincing when he asserts that an African language should be preferred to a European language as a substitute for the mother tongue of an African child:

L'avantage de substituer une langue africaine plutôt qu'une langue européenne à la langue maternelle des élèves tient au fait qu'elle est souvent très proche de celle-ci, ou sinon, que les expressions et les images employées se rattachent au monde africain et non à l'européen; l'élève n'est pas arraché au sol natal, mais amené à croître dans un terrain natal elargi; la langue est acquise au contact d'autres africains et non pas seulement en classe et dans les livres comme le serait une langue européenne. (p. 155)

(The advantage of using an African language as a substitute for the mother tongue of [African] pupils stems from the fact that the former will be close to the latter. The expressions and images used are African rather than European; the pupil is not uprooted from his/her native soil, but brought up in an extended home environment. The language is acquired in contact with other Africans, and not only in the classroom and in books as would be the case with a European language.)

To come back to our historical sketch, in 1954 when TANU (Tanganyika African National Union) was formed with the aim of fighting for Tanganyika's independence, the political leaders had in Kiswahili an important weapon for mobilising and uniting the people from all the ethnic groups in the country. Unlike in many other African countries, in Tanganyika politicians rarely had any need for interpreters during the campaign for independence and after, because Kiswahili was understood all over the country. This in turn enhanced the status of the language after independence, for it was now rightly regarded as the national language.

With this historical background, we are now in a position to consider the language situation in Tanzania today.

Language Use in Tanzania Today

Whereas only about 10% of the population of Tanzania speak Kiswahili as their mother tongue, it is estimated that about 90% of the population are bilingual in Kiswahili and a vernacular language (Abdulaziz, 1971). In contrast, only about 15% have any knowledge of English (Abdulaziz-Mkilifi, 1972). However, even for Kiswahili the pattern and extent of bilingualism is not uniform. O'Barr (1976) points out three distinct trends in the knowledge of Kiswahili in Tanzania, based on a survey he carried out in Pare District (North-East Tanzania):

1. Men almost universally tend to have some knowledge of Kiswahili.
2. Younger people have greater facility in using Kiswahili than older people.
3. The more literate and educated a person is, the more likely he is to be a fluent speaker of Kiswahili.

To this, one might add the urban–rural dichotomy. Kiswahili tends to be spoken more in urban areas than in rural areas. In fact, most children born in urban areas speak Kiswahili as their first language, even if their parents are not native speakers of Kiswahili. Again, there is the coast–interior dichotomy. The language is more widely spoken along the coast (where it originates) than in the interior of the country. Kiswahili is also likely to be spoken more widely in areas with a strong Islamic influence, like Tabora in Central Tanzania and Kigoma to the West, because these were centres of trade in the nineteenth century and consequently had more contact with Kiswahili-speaking traders from the coast.

Abdulaziz-Mkilifi (1972: 198) uses the term 'triglossia' to describe the pattern of language use in Tanzania:

A typical triglossia situation would be found where there exists side by side:

(a) regional or vernacular languages whose basic role is in oral intra-group communication;

(b) a local standardized *lingua franca* which is used extensively in the education system, mass media and in government administration but which is not developed enough to cover all settings of a modern urban technological culture; and

(c) a world language.

What this means in the case of Tanzania is: for those who speak a vernacular language, Kiswahili and English, each of these languages has its domains of use. The vernacular is usually the language of intimacy, i.e. of the home and close friends in informal situations. When people do not speak the same vernacular, then Kiswahili takes over the functions of the vernacular. Kiswahili is also the language of national public life: parliament, political rallies, post office, transport, banking, schools, church, etc. English is the language of higher education, the High Court and the Court of Appeal, diplomacy, foreign trade and any other business dealing with foreigners or foreign countries.

This pattern, however, is changing. The trend is that many domains where English was used are now being taken over by Kiswahili. Also, Kiswahili is not confined within the borders of Tanzania. It is spoken widely in Kenya, Uganda, Zaire, Rwanda, Burundi, and to some extent in Mozambique, Zambia, Somalia and the Sudan. Outside East Africa it is already being taught in the Universities of Guinea (Conakry), Rwanda, Burundi, Khartoum and Port Harcourt (Khamisi, 1980). So, although we cannot claim that Kiswahili is a world language, at least there is some justification for regarding it as an inter-African language.

A fairly comprehensive profile of language use in Tanzania is already available elsewhere (Polomé & Hill, 1980). In Table 2.1 we can only summarise, in a simplified form, the major domains of language use to demonstrate the triglossia situation in Tanzania.

TABLE 2.1 *Language use in different domains in Tanzania*

Domain	Vernacular	Kiswahili	English
1. Informal			
– home	VV	(VV)	
– with neighbours	(VV)	VV	
– work place	(V)	VV	
2. Cultural			
– place of worship	(V)	VV	
– literature		VV	V
– cinema		V	VV
3. Commercial			
– big business		VV	VV
– small business	(V)	VV	
– tourism		V	VV
4. Educational			
– medium: primary school	(V)	VV	
– medium: secondary school		(V)	VV
– medium: tertiary level			VV
– medium: adult education		VV	
– books, journals, etc.		VV	VV
5. Political			
– Parliament		VV	
– public rallies		VV	
6. Administration			
– village	(V)	VV	
– district/regional		VV	
– national		VV	(V)
7. Judiciary			
– Primary Court	(V)	VV	
– District Court	(V)	VV	(V)
– R.M.C.[a]	(V)	(VV)	VV
– High/Appeal Court	(V)	(VV)	VV
8. Mass media			
– radio		VV	V
– daily papers		VV	VV
9. International			
– diplomacy		(V)[b]	VV
– trade		(V)[b]	VV
– cultural exchange		(V)[b]	VV
– information exchange		(V)[b]	VV
– science and technology		(V)[b]	VV

KEY
[a] R.M.C. = Resident Magistrate's Court. [b] Used sometimes in dealing with neighbouring countries. VV Normal working language. V Sometimes used. ( ) Depends on setting, interlocutors, etc.
Source: Adapted from B. Misana (personal notes)

From Table 2.1 I would like to isolate language use in the judiciary and look at it in some detail because it illustrates the tri-focal nature of language use in Tanzania. The judiciary is especially interesting because it shows the trend of using Kiswahili, out of necessity, even where the official language is supposed to be English. Kavugha & Bobb (1980) give some interesting statistics about the use of language in the law courts in Tanzania. Table 2.2 shows the frequency of use of the different languages at different levels of the legal system.

TABLE 2.2 *Language use by type of court in Tanzania in 1970 (%)*

	High Court	R.M.C.	District Court	Primary Court
Kiswahili	28	56	79	92
English	60	43	15	00
Vernaculars	12	01	06	08

Source: Kavugha & Bobb, 1980: 232

Perhaps the figures in Table 2.2 do not tell us much apart from the fact that the higher you go in the hierarchy, the greater the use of English. The authors also note that the totals for the entire country show that Kiswahili is used for 78% of the time in court, English for 16% and vernaculars for 6% of the total time. More revealing, though, are these three observations (Kavugha & Bobb, 1980: 233, 237):

1. English was used by court personnel (judges, advocates, clerks) in 93.5% of the situations; and by witnesses, accused and plaintiffs in only 6.5% of the situations.

2. In 74.5% of the situations all the speakers knew Kiswahili because they were Tanzanians, Kenyans or Asians living in Tanzania. Only 5.55% could not use Kiswahili in the court situation.

3. Language switching (i.e. code-switching) seems to have occurred in all types of situations, and was used by all types of individuals regardless of rank, origin or level of education. Most (code) switching occurred between English and Kiswahili.

It seems, then, that in courts of law Kiswahili is the predominant language, especially in the lower courts. Vernaculars are used by those, especially in remote rural areas, who cannot speak Kiswahili. English, on the other hand, is spoken a lot in the High Court, even if the judges, the prosecutors and the defence counsels can speak Kiswahili. But, because these are often dealing with non-English speakers (accused, witnesses, plaintiffs) they are forced at times to speak Kiswahili and/or switch between English and Kiswahili.

There are several reasons why this situation prevails in Tanzanian law courts. First, as mentioned earlier, there are still some people in the rural areas who cannot speak Kiswahili. These will invariably use their vernacular in court, and they will need the services of an interpreter. Secondly (as far as the use of English is concerned) the Tanzanian legal system is modelled on the English legal system. Most of the laws are not only written in English but are also based on English law; judges and magistrates have to refer to English cases for precedent; those trained for the legal profession are trained in English for a legal system which is basically English-oriented. Thirdly, there are still a few legal experts in Tanzania who cannot speak Kiswahili, though their number is diminishing fast as Tanzanians replace foreigners in the legal profession. One would guess that today probably over 90% of those in the legal profession in Tanzania can speak Kiswahili. This implies that Kiswahili is even more widely used in court today than the statistics above (which reflect the situation in 1970) suggest.

It would be interesting to see how the picture in Tables 2.1 and 2.2 will have changed, say, 20 years from now. It is very difficult to predict, but there is a possibility that the vernaculars will gradually be pushed from the official functions where they are now used (out of necessity) as more and more people learn Kiswahili, and will be confined mainly to the informal domain. At the same time, English is also likely to give way to Kiswahili as the latter becomes more developed and therefore more able to cope with the modern world. However, English is likely to remain an important tool in higher education as a 'library language', as well as a medium of international communication.

References

ABDULAZIZ, M.H. 1971, Tanzania's national language policy and the rise of Swahili political culture. In W.H. WHITELEY (ed.) *Language Use and Social Change.* Oxford: Oxford University Press.
ABDULAZIZ-MKILIFI, M.H. 1972, Triglossia and Swahili — English bilingualism in Tanzania. *Language in Society* 1, 2.
CAMERON, J. and DODD, W. 1970, *Society, Schools and Progress in Tanzania.* Oxford: Pergamon Press.
KAVUGHA, D. and BOBB, D. 1980, The use of language in the Law Courts in Tanzania. In E. POLOMÉ and C.P. HILL (eds) *Language in Tanzania.* Oxford: Oxford University Press.
KHAMISI, A.M. 1980, Language Planning and the Use of Mother-Tongue in

Education: The Case of Tanzania. Paper presented at the UNESCO training seminar, Lomé, Togo, September 1980.

MAZRUI, A.A. and ZIRIMU, P. 1978, Church, state, and the marketplace in the spread of Kiswahili. In B. SPOLSKY and R. COOPER (eds) *Case Studies in Bilingual Education*. Rowley, Mass.: Newbury House.

MOUMOUNI, A. 1967, *L'education en Afrique*. Paris: Francois Maspero.

O'BARR, W.M. 1976, Language use and language policy in Tanzania: An overview. In W.M. O'BARR and J.F. O'BARR (eds) *Language and Politics*. The Hague: Mouton.

POLOMÉ, E. and HILL, C.P. (eds) 1980, *Language in Tanzania*. Oxford: Oxford University Press.

WHITELEY, W.H. 1969, *Swahili: The Rise of a National Language*. London: Methuen.

3 On the history of English Language Teaching in Tanzania: Three theses

A.F. LWAITAMA, C.M. RUBAGUMYA and M.K. KAPINGA

Introduction

The purpose of this chapter is to present, in outline form, three theses on the history of English Language Teaching (henceforth ELT) in Tanzania. We feel that it is time special encouragement was given to the systematic study of the history of Foreign Languages Teaching (henceforth FLT) in general and ELT in particular, especially now that ELT has assumed such a high significance in Tanzanian educational planning and practice (Rubagumya, 1986; Schmied, 1986; Trappes-Lomax, this volume). Schmied (1986: 72) summarises the facts relating to this significance when he states that:

> In general, the precarious position of English in Tanzanian education in the 1980's can be summarised as a *growing divergence between curriculum and reality on the societal level and between language needs and language competence on the individual level.* (Our emphasis)

A systematic study of the history of ELT in Tanzania should be of great assistance to those wishing to find adequate explanations for some of the 'paradoxes'[1] in Tanzanian educational planning in general and language policy evolution in particular.

Summary of the Theses

The three theses we wish to present are:

(a) That before the advent of British Colonial rule in 1919, ELT had

15

not acquired 'improper'[2] privileges for itself and that it was then possible to conceive of it as an 'endogenous'[3] and 'differentiated'[4] operation.

(b) That the first republican phase of the post-independence era (Mlahagwa, 1986: 3) has set in motion socio-economic processes which have eroded and are bound to continue to erode the 'improper' privileges which ELT acquired for itself in the second phase of Tanzania's colonial epoch.

(c) That to the extent to which Tanzania succeeds in overcoming the negative aspects of its colonial legacy, to that extent will ELT in Tanzania evolve in the direction of its being conceived of, once more, as an 'endogenous' and 'differentiated' operation stripped of many of its former 'improper' privileges.

We will now discuss each of these theses in summary form before offering a relatively extended discussion of the third thesis in the next major section of the chapter.

The First Thesis

A summary of the First Thesis could be that the first, second and third epochs of Tanzania's socio-economic history (as proposed by Mlahagwa, 1986: 3–4)[5] were characterised by a conception of ELT (and FLT in general) which was 'endogenous' and 'differentiated'. In contrast to this, the thesis will claim that it was in the fourth epoch (for FLT in general) and the second phase of that epoch (for ELT in particular) when 'exogenous' and 'undifferentiated' conceptions of FLT/ELT emerged. It will further be claimed that it was the acquisition of 'improper' privileges by first German and later English which occasioned these strange conceptions.

A detailed exposition of the First Thesis would involve description of the first contacts between foreigners and indigenous peoples and the form these initial contacts took. With respect to ELT, a contrastive appraisal would be required of ELT in the days of British missionary work before the advent of British rule in 1919, and ELT in both mission and state schools after 1919.

The emergence of Kiswahili as a language which has over the years acquired 'proper' privileges for itself will also need further discussion (Kapinga, 1984: 19–28; Rubagumya, this volume). It was this emergence of Kiswahili as an indigenous *lingua franca* which prompted some of the attempts by the British colonial state functionaries to accord ELT 'improper' privileges in the sphere of national language planning. Rubagumya (this volume) reports on the views of such representatives of British colonial rule in the region as Bishop Tucker of Uganda and the 1953 Binns Mission Report; these views reflect the general conceptions of ELT which must have been widely shared then by the colonial state functionaries.

The main thrust of the First Thesis is that ELT was once conceived of as an 'endogenous' and 'differentiated' operation; and that it was the 'improper' privileges accorded the English language in the period of British colonial rule that resulted in the emergence of a perception of ELT as an 'exogenous' and 'undifferentiated' operation.

The Second Thesis

In the Second Thesis of this chapter we are arguing that ELT in Tanzania is passing through an inevitable crisis-ridden transition phase. This is the phase when ELT is still conceived of as an 'exogenous' and 'undifferentiated' operation, even though the 'improper' privileges accorded to the English language which occasioned such a conception have been and continue to be eroded away. The first republican phase of Tanzania's post-independence era (1962–72) has witnessed some 'significant reordering of both the economic foundations of society and the superstructure' (Mlahagwa, 1986: 3). A situation in which out of a population of 10 million in 1962 the country had only '12 African civil engineers, no mechanical or electrical engineers, 5 chemists, 1 forester, 9 veterinary surgeons, 8 telecommunication technicians, no geologists, and only 38 Africans among 600 graduate secondary school teachers' (Chonjo, 1985: 18) was bound to be unacceptable to any post-colonial Tanzanian state.

A situation like that at independence in 1961 whereby '[the] manufacturing sector establishments employed a total of 20,000 persons which for a population of about 9 million (in 1961) catered for the livelihood of about one per cent of the population' (Wangwe, 1986: 1–2) was also bound to be unacceptable.

Many of 'the developments in the Tanzanian educational system in the post independence period leading to the Declarations of Arusha and Musoma' (Chonjo, 1985: 17–19) cannot be understood except in the light of the points raised above. When '85% of all jobs requiring a University degree are occupied by non-Africans', as was the situation at independence, one can understand why an exogenous and undifferentiated conception of ELT was only possible during British colonial rule!

An extended discussion of the Second Thesis would require an appraisal of all the attempts that are being made to maintain 'artificially' the
'improper' privileges that English was accorded by the colonial authorities
(Criper & Dodd, 1984; Trappes-Lomax, this volume). It would also require
an appraisal of the socio-economic processes which continue to erode the
'improper' privileges that English enjoys in spite of official attempts to stem
the tide. The recent major expansions in secondary school access; the
continuing influence of manpower and localisation planning on tertiary
(especially University) entry processes; and the continuing failure of plans
to stem the tide of rural–urban migration are offered as such socio-
economic processes.

As Lwaitama (1986: 34) has put it:

People in factories and offices have holidays — paid leave they call it.
They have pensions. They have greater independence from control by
their parents and relatives. I hear that in Europe people are paid for
quite long periods of time for doing nothing! Who would not like a life
like that? . . . The Europeans who come over here are always found
enjoying themselves in our hotels in our own country! Who would not
like a life like they lead?

These are the sentiments which reflect on the socio-economic imperatives of
this epoch of Tanzanian history. It is these imperatives which will gradually
force Tanzanians to overcome the colonial prejudices which underlie the
conception of ELT as an 'exogenous' and 'undifferentiated' operation. To
'develop' in such a European sense will require the acquisition of science
and technology (Chonjo, 1986) by all the people of Tanzania, which
acquisition will prove impossible to organise except in Kiswahili and
through an endogenous and differentiated conception of FLT, together
with ELT.

The Third Thesis

This thesis offers a prognosis of how ELT is likely to be conceived of
and practised when Tanzania has overcome many of its negative colonial
legacies. By and large, discussion here centres on what constitutes an
endogenous and differentiated conception of FLT in general and ELT in
particular. In the next section of the chapter we give a relatively extended
discussion of this third thesis. More specifically, we endeavour to give some
explanation of what we mean by the term 'endogenous' and the term
'differentiated'.

Extended discussion of the third thesis

In this discussion of the Third Thesis, three points are emphasised. The first point is that we are convinced that a conception of ELT as an endogenous and differentiated operation will in time become the dominant conception. Our conviction in this regard derives from two sources.

The first source is that we find no evidence for doubting the correctness of the observation by M.I. Isayev (1977: 394) who has stated that: 'It is expected that during the next several decades the relative weight of publications in English, French and German will decline while that of publications in Japanese, Hindi, Arabic and Swahili will increase.' As adult education programmes worldwide succeed in drawing into the literary world peoples who previously were left out of educational programmes, the importance of publications in the more than 2.5 thousand world languages will increase. Where previously only élite groups and élite languages dominated the literary scene, in time these imbalances in the reproduction of world knowledge will be corrected.

This leads us to the second source of our conviction that the endogenous and differentiated conception of FLT is bound to prevail. We believe that Tanzania is an economically backward part of the world's 'market economy system' or capitalism. We also believe that this 'world market economy system' is today in what Polish theologian Paulos Mar Gregorios (1985: 5) has termed a state of 'panic'. It is in this state of panic because 'four disturbing trends of the eighties' make it so. These four trends are: 'stagnant production, growing unemployment, shrinking world trade and the growing debt burden of the developing countries'.

We believe that a world which allows its economically backward parts to starve of food when there are food mountains in its developed parts; a world which allows its economically backward parts to be starved of 'development' finance when the commercial banks of its developed parts are 'overflowing with liquid credit and looking around for borrowers' (Gregorios, 1985: 5); we believe that such a world will gradually force the peoples of countries like Tanzania to look again at the ideology of 'developmentalism' (Gregorios, 1985: 2) and at the 'undifferentiated' conception of FLT in general and ELT in particular.

An endogenous conception of ELT

The second point we wish to emphasise in this section, therefore, is that an 'endogenous' conception of ELT is called for. By this we mean that ELT needs to be seen as an operation whose goals and methods are determined by the proper socio-economic requirements of the people of Tanzania as a whole. In practical terms, it means that ELT needs to be planned and executed in a manner which facilitates the development of Kiswahili as the language of wider communication in the scientific and technological fields as much as it is in the social and political sphere. Such a conception of ELT is also likely to wish to use Kiswahili as the language of instruction in teaching English (Karugaba, 1985; Kapinga, in press). Teaching foreign languages through Kiswahili should enhance the use of Kiswahili as the language of 'language education' (Halliday, 1985).

An endogenous conception of ELT will wish to strengthen those practices which in the past have stressed the centrality of African literature in English in the development of English language teaching curricula. The experiences of Africans in the diaspora as they have been recorded in English in, for example, the songs of Bob Marley and the novels of Richard Wright, would partly constitute the form and content of such a conception of ELT.

The idea that English was intrinsically the 'chosen tongue' among all world languages is at variance with an endogenous conception of ELT. All 'improper' privileges accorded the English language in the past have at this stage withered away!

A 'differentiated' conception of ELT

The elaboration of our concept of a 'differentiated' conception of ELT is our last point in this section. By 'differentiated' we wish to refer to the idea that different people in Tanzania will need to acquire different 'target competencies' in the language for different purposes.

At this stage, gone will be the idea that all Tanzanian learners of English at whatever level had to aim at pronouncing English with an RP accent (Maghway, 1981: 19)! We are not actually certain that a differentiated conception of ELT would permit the introduction of English as a subject in primary schools as early as grade three, as is the practice at the moment (Rubagumya, 1986: 296–8).

A differentiated conception of ELT also implies that some Tanzanians may not need to have to learn English at any level. They may, instead, need to learn some other foreign language(s) such as Hausa, Arabic, Portuguese, Lingala, Sotho, Zulu, French or Chichewa.

Conclusion

In conclusion, we wish to recommend these three theses in outline to students of the history of Tanzania who have an interest in the relationship between language and politics (Alexandre, 1968; O'Barr, 1976; Leibowitz, 1976; Bretton, 1976; Polomé & Hill, 1980). We also recommend these theses to students of the history of ELT in general (Howatt, 1984; Bint, 1985; Naysmith, 1986; Picket, 1980).

As the debate about ELT in Tanzania continues, we recommend that participants in the debate acquaint themselves with these three theses. They are offered in the humble belief that the issues in the ELT debate are not likely to be resolved in favour of the wishes of those who seem to have an 'exogenous' and 'undifferentiated' conception of ELT and who seem to take the claims of the ideology of 'developmentalism' for granted.

We believe that all efforts that are being made at the official level to extend artificially the life of the 'improper' privileges which ELT acquired during the colonial period[6] are not likely to succeed in attaining their objectives (Criper & Dodd, 1984; Roy-Campbell, 1985; Trappes-Lomax, this volume). We believe such efforts are based on a misreading of the history and destiny of ELT in Tanzania.

Notes to Chapter 3

1. We do not believe there has been any clarification of national language policy towards ELT and Kiswahili as Dunn (1985: 44) appears to believe. We are of the opinion that statements attributed to former President Nyerere (*Mzalendo*, 28.10.1984) and to Minister for Education Makweta (*Uhuru*, 8.8.1983) (Dunn, 1985: 45 and Schmied, 1986: 108–9) provide possible explanations for the 'paradoxes' rather than clarify such 'paradoxes' and ambivalences. After all, Mr Makweta was the Chairman of the Presidential Commission on Education which had recommended in 1982 that 'as from January 1985, all classes in secondary school should be conducted in Kiswahili and envisaged that by 1992 all subjects at University level will be taught in Kiswahili' (Rubagumya, 1986: 284).

2. We use the term 'improper' to refer to those privileges which are not in accord with the proper place (of the language given such privileges) in terms of the domains of use of that language in the given society. 'Improper' is not here used as a term of abuse or a mere reflection of nationalist sentiments on our part against some foreign language. We are not against the according of special privileges to languages in general but rather the according of 'improper' privileges in the specific circumstances under discussion.

3. We use 'endogenous' here to refer to a conception of FLT whereby the target competencies in the target foreign language and the modalities of learning and teaching it are determined by a person or persons *indigenous to Tanzania* who is/ are the clients of the FLT operation. This is distinguished from the conception of FLT whereby the goals and means of FLT are established by some native speaker(s) of the target foreign language. The concept of the endogenous

teaching of a foreign language is currently being researched by one of the authors
of this chapter (Kapinga, 1986). Some elaboration of the concept is given in the
third section of this chapter (see also Roper, 1978).

4. By a 'differentiated' conception of FLT/ELT is meant the conception of
FLT/ELT where one does not set undifferentiated goals for the learning of a
particular foreign language for all the citizens of a particular country. To conceive
of ELT undifferentially is to assume that it is needed by everyone equally and that
it can be learnt by everyone at socially undifferentiated rates and levels.

5. Mlahagwa (1986: 2–3) states that:

Landmarks in the ensemble of relations of production are what is often
referred to in history as epoch or era. For the Tanzanian social formation five
major epochs can be identified: the epoch in which societies of this country had
not yet been incorporated into the Indian Ocean maritime trading system; the
epoch of the domination of merchant capital, especially that of the Portuguese;
the era of the domination of Oman Arabs along the coast and the tributary
state system in the interior; the imperialist colonial epoch; and the post-
independence era, of which the first phase of republican rule is the most
important period.
(See also Lwoga, 1986 and Meena, 1986.)

6. One such effort is reported to be the practice of punishing any secondary school
student who uses Kiswahili or any language other than English in informal
conversations within the school compound, in spite of the fact that Kiswahili (as a
subject) and Political Education (i.e. Current Affairs and the Political Economy
of Tanzania) are still taught in Kiswahili! The Catholic Weekly *Kiongozi* (e.g.
1985) publishes complaints by victims of such policies from time to time.

References

ALEXANDRE, P. 1968, Some linguistic problems of nation-building in Negro
    Africa. In J.A. FISHMAN, C.A. FERGUSON and J. GUPTA (eds) *Language
    Problems of Developing Nations* (pp. 119–27). New York: Wiley.
BINT, P. 1985, Review of Howatt, A.P.R.: *A History of English Language
    Teaching*, Oxford University Press 1984. In *Espmena* (Khartoum) No. 20
    (August), 38–41.
BRETTON, H.C. 1976, Political science, language and politics. In W.M. O'BARR
    and J.F. O'BARR (eds) *Language and Politics* (pp. 432–48). The Hague:
    Mouton.
CHONJO, P.N. 1985, *Secondary Technical Education and Industrial Development
    in Tanzania*. PhD Thesis, University of Southampton.
— 1986, Science and Technology Education: Why We Need It in Tanzania.
    Seminar paper: Department of Education, University of Dar es Salaam.
CRIPER, C. and DODD, W. 1984, *Report on The Teaching of English Language
    and Its Use as a Medium of Instruction in Tanzania*. Dar es Salaam: The
    British Council. (Mimeo.)
DUNN, A.S. 1985, Swahili policy implementation in Tanzania: The role of the
    National Swahili Council (Bakita). *Studies in the Linguistic Sciences* 15, 1,
    31–47.

GREGORIOS, P.M. 1985, Liberation and Development — A Christian Answer. Paper for a Christian Peace Conference 'Solidarity, Liberation and Development', 25–29 March 1985, Warsaw, Poland. (Mimeo.)

HALLIDAY, M.A.K. 1985, Language Across the Culture. SEAMEO RELC Conference Paper: Singapore. (Mimeo.)

HOWATT, A.P.R. 1984, *A History of English Language Teaching*. Oxford: Oxford University Press.

ISAYEV, M.I. 1977, *National Language in the USSR: Problems and Solutions*. Moscow: Progress Publishers.

KAPINGA, M.K. 1984, *The Shifting Sociolinguistic Tri-Focalism in Tanzania*. MA Thesis, University of Lancaster.

— 1986, Pattern of Integrative Motivation and the Endogenous Teaching of Foreign Languages. Research Notes. Department of Foreign Languages and Linguistics, University of Dar es Salaam. (Mimeo.)

— In press, *Naanza Kujifunza Kiingereza*. Tabora: Tanganyika Mission Press.

KARUGABA, S.R. 1985, *The Use of Kiswahili in the Teaching of English in Tanzanian Secondary Schools*. MA Thesis, University of Dar es Salaam.

kiongozi (Catholic Weekly) 1985, Kipingamizi cha Lugha (Editorial). Toleo la Kwanza — Oktoba, 1985 p. 2.

LEIBOWITZ, A.H. 1976, Language and the law: The exercise of political power through official designation of language. In W. O'BARR and J. O'BARR (eds) *Language and Politics*. The Hague: Mouton.

LWAITAMA, A.F. 1986, The Nyerere heritage. *Bulletin of Tanzanian Affairs* (London), No. 25, September, pp. 32–35.

LWOGA, C.M.F. 1986, Development Plans and Rural Development Strategies in Tanzania 1961–1981: A Critical Review. Paper presented at the Historical Association of Tanzania 20th Anniversary, 15–20 September, University of Dar es Salaam. (Mimeo.)

MAGHWAY, J.B. 1981, Tanzanian speakers of English: Effects of spelling on vowel pronunciation. *Language and Linguistics* 1, 19–55.

MEENA, R. 1986, Is SADCC learning from Historical Experience? Paper presented to the Historical Association of Tanzania 20th Anniversary, 15–20 September, University of Dar es Salaam. (Mimeo.)

MLAHAGWA, J.R. 1986, The Historicity of the First Phase of the Republic of Tanzania. Paper presented to the Historical Association of Tanzania 20th Anniversary, 15–20 September, University of Dar es Salaam. (Mimeo.)

NAYSMITH, J. 1986, English as imperialism. *ITEFL Newsletter* No. 92 (August), p. 3.

O'BARR, W.M. 1976, Language use and language policy in Tanzania: An overview. In W.M. O'BARR and J. O'BARR (eds) *Language and Politics*. The Hague: Mouton.

PICKET, D. 1980, Getting English into perspective. In *ELT Documents 108: National Syllabuses*, British Council (London), pp. 54–73.

POLOMÉ, E.C. and HILL, C.P. (eds) 1980, *Language in Tanzania*. Oxford: Oxford University Press.

ROPER, N. 1978, *Pocket Medical Dictionary*. Edinburgh: Longman.

ROY-CAMPBELL, Z.M. 1985, Teaching English as a medium of instruction: An integrative approach. *Studies in Curriculum Development* No. 3 (June).

RUBAGUMYA, C.M. 1986, Language planning in the Tanzanian educational system: Problems and prospects. *Journal of Multilingual and Multicultural Development* 7, 4, 283–300.

SCHMIED, J.J. 1986, English in Tanzanian education. *Bayreuth African Studies Series* No. 5, pp. 63–114.
WANGWE, S.M. 1986, Industrialization Experiences in Tanzania 1961–1985. Paper presented to the Historical Association of Tanzania 20th Anniversary, 15–20 September, University of Dar es Salaam. (Mimeo.)

4 Reflections on recent developments in language policy in Tanzania

J.M. RUGEMALIRA, C.M. RUBAGUMYA, M.K. KAPINGA,
A.F. LWAITAMA and J.G. TETLOW

Introduction

While an International Conference on the use of Kiswahili at the meetings of the Organisation of African Unity was going on in Zanzibar in mid-December 1986, a group of linguists at the University of Dar es Salaam was holding a workshop on bilingualism.[1] The workshop was organised under the auspices of the Department of Foreign Languages and Linguistics and was led by Dr Marilyn Martin-Jones from the University of Lancaster (UK).

During the course of the workshop we discussed a wide range of issues relating to bilingualism, but we paid special attention to the nature and extent of bilingualism among pupils and students in all sectors of education in Tanzania. We revisited the debate about the media of instruction in the schools and colleges and noted that the arguments on either side (Kiswahili vs. English) have not always been sufficiently grasped by the protagonists. We examined recent policy developments and concluded that at this level the case for Kiswahili was currently being put very weakly, if at all.

When considering the actual day to day practice in the educational institutions in the country, the group noted that Kiswahili is unceremoniously taking over as the only viable medium of learning for young Tanzanian people. We contemplated the consequences of this discrepancy between official policy prescriptions and the actual needs of the language users for the development of Kiswahili and for the general quality of education.

The following is a result of our deliberations. It is our statement, as concerned linguists and educationalists, on the language question in our education system. We maintain that the switch from English to Kiswahili as the medium of learning in the secondary schools is long overdue. We argue that despite protestations to the contrary the continued dominance of English as a prestige language in the education system is bound to hamper the development of Kiswahili in the academic fields. We show why a rescue operation like the four-year English Language Support Project cannot, by itself, reinstate English as an effective language of education in Tanzania. We contend that without a change of heart on the part of policy makers, Tanzania will end up with the worst of both worlds, at least in the short term — developing neither Kiswahili nor English as an effective medium of teaching and learning.

We hope that by making our position known to a wider public, especially learners and teachers in schools and colleges, we can keep the debate alive. But we also hope that the policy makers will heed our call. In any case nobody should accuse us of silent collusion in the stultification of Kiswahili and the failure to evolve a meaningful education system.

Recent Language Policy Developments in Tanzania

For almost 20 years, it has been the national policy in Tanzania to replace English by Kiswahili as a medium of learning at all educational levels. Reaffirmation of this policy and plans to implement it have been made at more or less regular intervals — 1969, 1970, 1974, 1979, 1982 (Trappes-Lomax, this volume). The argument for the change from English to Kiswahili was succinctly put in the 1969/74 Plan:

> We have a system where the medium of instruction in primary schools is Kiswahili, while in secondary schools it is English. This constitutes an educational problem and potentially a dangerous situation. It will create a class of those educated in Kiswahili medium and another educated in English medium. It will render secondary education irrelevant to the problems of the masses . . . It will not be justified to continue to offer secondary education in English. (Quoted in Mlama & Matteru, 1978: 5)

This argument is even more valid today than it was in 1969, in view of the mushrooming private secondary schools, most of which are purported to be technical/vocational schools. But, almost two decades later, the policy has still not been implemented. In fact, it has been stated categorically that English will continue to be the medium of instruction in secondary schools. To implement this new policy, a programme based on the Criper and Dodd recommendations (Criper & Dodd, 1984) to 'rehabilitate' English in

Tanzanian secondary schools has now taken off. The stated aim of this programme is to help to make English an effective medium of instruction.

It is interesting to note that the main reason officially given for maintaining English as a medium of instruction is that Tanzania must not be isolated from the rest of the world. Since English is a world language, it is argued, we must use it as a medium of education in order to keep abreast with what is going on elsewhere in the world. In the words of the former Minister of Education: 'We must learn from foreign nations and in order to do so we must use English to promote understanding [of what is learnt] in schools' (quoted in Schmied, 1986: 109). Obviously the assumption here is that to be able to use English for international communication, we must also use it as a medium of instruction. In other words, underlying the argument in favour of English as the medium of education is the belief that this will necessarily lead to greater proficiency in English among secondary school pupils in Tanzania. However, it has recently been argued that this is not likely to be the case, given the present sociolinguistic environment in Tanzania (Rubagumya, 1986). Nor is English likely to facilitate learning, as implied by the Minister's statement quoted above.

It is also unlikely that the English Language Support Project based on the Criper and Dodd recommendations will make a significant change in secondary school pupils' proficiency in English language. The four-year programme seems to be a short-term 'stop-gap' operation. What will happen after the four years remains unclear. There does not seem to be any long-term plan to overhaul the teaching of English.

The budget for this programme (financed by Britain's Overseas Development Administration) is to be in the region of £2 million. 'The English Language Support Project will include 20 scholarships in Britain for English teachers, seminars, regular consignments of new books from Britain to include English course-books and sets of class readers, class libraries and audio-visual equipment' (*Daily News*, December, 1986). So a set of scholarships each year, a couple of course-books and sets of class readers (most of which are, to say the least, irrelevant to Tanzania) are supposed to bring about this 'miracle' and make English an efficient medium of instruction! In addition, the recommendation that schools should encourage, or even force, pupils to use English outside the class-room is unrealistic. How is the 'speak English' rule to be enforced? This is in operation in some schools already. Do the teachers themselves always speak English outside or even inside the classroom? In any case, supposing it were possible to force pupils and teachers to use English at all times within the school compound, and of course punishing them if they did not, what would be the political and cultural implications of this?

It would seem to us, therefore, that the decision to retain English as a medium of instruction is based on ill-founded assumptions, and that the present measures taken to 'rehabilitate' English are insufficient in the long term for improving standards of English language teaching across the educational system. In the following section we present what, in our view, is a strong case for Kiswahili. In the process we answer the main objections put forward against the use of Kiswahili as a potential medium of instruction in secondary education in Tanzania.

The Case for Kiswahili

It is beyond dispute that the educational process in any society ought to be conducted through a language that both the learner and the teacher command well. This is a minimum requirement for any communication to take place in the teaching/learning situation. In addition, at a more general level, the language of education should be that which is accessible to the majority of the population. This facilitates the generation of knowledge and its dissemination to as wide an audience as possible within a given society. When it comes to the choice of a medium of education these are the two basic considerations. Thus the French do not educate their children through the English language, they use French; similarly, the British use English, the Chinese use Chinese, etc. For Tanzanians (Waswahili) the appropriate choice is Kiswahili. It is the language that the majority of learners can manipulate at a relatively early age. It is the language that is most accessible to the Tanzanian population at large; no other language — Sukuma, Chaga, Nyakyusa, Haya, Gogo, Maasai, English, etc. — can challenge Kiswahili on these two counts.

English is a case in point. Several studies (cf. Mvungi, 1974; Mlama & Matteru, 1978; Criper & Dodd, 1984) have amply shown that English has ceased to be an effective medium of education in Tanzanian secondary schools. For instance, on the basis of a test administered to 2,410 learners drawn from all levels of the education system, Criper & Dodd (1984) made the following observations:

. . . throughout their secondary school career little or no other subject information is getting across to about 50% of the pupils in our sample. Only about 10% of Form IV's are at a level at which one might expect English medium education to *begin*. (p. 14)

. . . the proportion of [Form V] pupils at level 'A' (nearing but not at independent reading level) is still small — 17%. (p. 14)

. . . [University] students' level of English is substantially below that required for University English medium study. (p. 15)

. . . less than 20% of the [University] sample tested were at a level where they would find it easy to read even the simpler books required for their academic studies. (p. 43)

. . . we estimate that perhaps up to 75% of teaching, at any rate in Form 1, is being done through Kiswahili. (p. 34)

These statements will not surprise anyone acquainted with the educational process in Tanzania. The situation is a logical consequence of the successive narrowing down of the sphere of English in Tanzanian society over the last two decades. The effect has been that the language is no longer a second language, but a foreign language. This means that English is a language which only a small proportion of Tanzanians use, and this mainly in communicating with foreigners rather than with fellow Tanzanians. English is not the language used to address the bus conductor, to enquire about a balance at the bank, to ask for stamps at the post office, to reserve a seat at the railway station, to speak to the medical assistant at the health centre, to buy an allocation of 'essential commodities' at the 'Kaya' shop, or to make a statement at the police station. Nor is English the language spoken by Members of Parliament while debating a bill. The Tanzanian learner encounters English only in the classroom. As soon as he/she sets foot outside the classroom the learner is at home in a predominantly Swahili environment. These conditions are not conducive to the attainment, by every learner, of the required level of proficiency in English.

A rescue operation to restore English to its glorious past cannot create the crucial conditions necessary to make Tanzanians accept and use English as a second language. To give English such a status would require, among other things, a major shift in attitudes and values with respect to language. It would require that not only should the government declare a compulsory squeeze on the spheres already taken over by Kiswahili, but also that the majority of Tanzanians actually accept such a reduction of the range of domains in which Kiswahili is currently used. In practical terms Tanzanians would have to use English in more of their daily activities than is the case today. But no government, however totalitarian, could effect such a change! Requiring staff and students to speak English in the school compound is high-handed enough. But how effective can this directive be? To allocate six months of Form 1 to a foreign language is generous enough. But what returns can be reasonably expected? Clearly the current English Language Support Project funded by the British Government is aiming to do the impossible — to restore English as an effective language of education in Tanzania by giving it the status of a second language.

Besides the above pedagogical considerations, the case for Kiswahili also has a cultural/nationalistic aspect. The adoption of the language as medium will enhance its status and promote its further development. The present restriction on Kiswahili serves to perpetuate the impression that the language cannot be employed in advanced academic discourse. The ban on speaking Kiswahili both in the classroom and the school compound in general serves to create the impression in the learner's young mind that it is shameful and criminal to speak Kiswahili, that the language is not respectable.

A major objection to Kiswahili has traditionally been the supposed inadequacy of the language with regard to technical terminology. Some people even take the view that certain concepts cannot be expressed in Kiswahili. It should be noted that to the extent that human beings can express their experience through language then any language can be used. In this regard no language is inherently inadequate. Living languages continuously change to accommodate developments experienced by the relevant speakers. The most obvious of such changes is the acquisition, by borrowing or inventing, of new vocabulary terms: witness the numerous Latin, Greek and French terms borrowed by English! Here necessity is the mother of invention; as long as a need to express something exists, a way of expressing it *will* inevitably be found by the speakers. In the case of Kiswahili current policy places barriers in the way of such needs arising. The significant amount of terminology that already exists is confined to the drawers and shelves of language specialists. Young learners go through primary school using Kiswahili terms; the few who go on to secondary school never have the opportunity to build on that base. Instead, they acquire a new set of terms to designate the new concepts they encounter in different subjects across the secondary curriculum.

Like an inventory of technical terms, Kiswahili teaching materials can only be accumulated through a process of actually using the language and thereby creating a need for such materials. Under present conditions no secondary school materials in Kiswahili can be produced since no audience exists for them. No writer will invest time, nor publisher risk money, in such a venture. The Institute of Education will go on producing a few materials in English, while we go on importing most books.

The majority of teachers at secondary and tertiary levels are proficient in Kiswahili and should thus be able to use the language in teaching with a short orientation programme. Certainly it is *not* the case that Tanzanian teachers are more at ease teaching in English than in Kiswahili. They may hesitate about the Swahili technical terminology, but the language issue cannot be reduced to a question of terminology. The few English-speaking expatriate teachers, on the other hand, should be required to learn Kiswahili. This means that instead of requiring Tanzanian learners to master English to accommodate expatriate teachers, the latter should learn Kiswahili to meet the learners' needs. Many expatriates from non-anglophone countries who learn English in order to take up a job in Tanzania would, instead, learn Kiswahili.

A further objection to Kiswahili has been that the language does not have the same international role as English and that its adoption as the language of the secondary school would close Tanzania's 'window to the outside world', with the effect that Tanzanians would lose track of techno-logical developments. Two observations are pertinent here. First, it needs to be demonstrated that every Tanzanian who goes to school *can* and *needs to* master a foreign language. Or to use the same metaphor as above, it must be shown that it is both necessary and possible for every Tanzanian to look through the same 'window'. Second, it should be demonstrated that countries such as Finland, Norway, China or Japan, which do not teach their children through the medium of an 'international' language, are isolated and have lost track of technological developments beyond their borders. The persistence of English-medium education owes a great deal to the rarely expressed belief that this situation guarantees English a hold on Tanzanian society. The fear is that once English loses the role of medium of education then nobody will pay attention to it any longer. This was explicitly stated by former President Nyerere while addressing members of the association of Kiswahili writers (UKUTA): 'Mwalimu urged Tanzanians to hold on to both English and Kiswahili and added that English is the language of instruction in secondary schools and colleges because if it is kept as merely a subject it might die' (*Mzalendo*, 28.10.1984; our translation).

But the policy of maintaining a hold for English, at whatever cost, cannot be justified and, moreover, it has not worked. Kiswahili has been expanding its realm into education, albeit slowly, almost stealthily because of administrative barriers. English has ceased to be an effective medium of teaching and learning. Educational standards have accordingly suffered. Do we need further proof before we accept the fact that the *use* of English at school is not the crucial condition for successful acquisition of the language by Tanzanian learners? Some countries that are smaller than Tanzania, e.g. Holland, Denmark, Finland, require their children to learn a foreign language. They do not, however, use a foreign language in teaching mathematics or history to their children. Can't we learn a lesson from these countries?

In summary, we have argued that Kiswahili is the language most suited for the role of medium of education in Tanzania, that English has *de facto* lost this role irrecoverably, and that the supposed inadequacies of Kiswahili will be overcome only if the language is put to use and allowed to develop faster. In view of this we would like to make the following recommendations.

Recommendations

We take it that recommendations can be understood in three senses. First, there are courses of action that can be recommended in general terms. Take, for example, the recommendations found in the monograph edited by Trappes-Lomax, Besha & Mcha entitled *Changing Language Media*, published in 1982 by the Department of Foreign Languages and Linguistics of the University of Dar es Salaam. There are also courses of action that one can advise the educational planners and policy makers to adopt; these are recommendations requiring immediate government attention. Finally, there are courses of action one would wish to advise interested individuals and institutions to begin to follow without waiting for policy clarity on the part of government.

We offer recommendations of all three kinds below.

General recommendations

Ten general recommendations are offered. It is recommended:

1. That Kiswahili begin to be used as a medium of instruction in secondary schools in all subjects from 1989. (This should be facilitated by students' familiarity with some specific terminology introduced in Kiswahili in upper grades of primary education.)

2. That code-switching between Kiswahili and English when references are made to technical terms should be seen as a natural, i.e. 'normal', expression of this particular stage of the evolution of Tanzanian educational bilingualism. (Teachers and students should not be unreasonably rebuked when they code-switch nor should they be made to feel inadequate in any way for such code-switching. There is ample evidence that code-switching

involves considerable verbal skill.)

3. That the Institute of Education should be responsible for co-ordinating efforts in developing Kiswahili-medium teaching materials. Subject panels also should be strengthened and encouraged to assist the Institute in this regard.

4. That conferences/workshops bringing together interested parties in the Eastern African region should be held from time to time to enhance dialogue and consultations among linguists and educationalists. This should help in guarding against national parochialism and isolationism.

5. That the role of ordinary teachers in the process of curriculum change should be enhanced. Conferences/workshops/seminars involving such teachers at district, regional and zonal level should be encouraged.

6. That the new Kiswahili terminologies should be disseminated as widely as possible. Lists of such terminology produced by as many bodies as possible should be made available to as many interested parties as possible. (BAKITA (National Kiswahili Council) and TUKI (Institute of Kiswahili Research) should, of course, co-ordinate this.)

7. That refresher courses in the Department of Education should be organised in collaboration with the Institute of Education and the Ministry of Education. The flow of information on the process of media change between teachers, education administrators and University academics must be maximised.

8. That the implications of the media change with respect to the administration of national examinations must be worked out in advance. Educational bodies like the National Examination Council and the Institute of Education must work more closely to effect the smooth implementation of the media change.

9. That teaching methodology should be viewed as broadly as possible and should involve the use of a wide range of resources, e.g. supplementary readers, work-sheets, tape-recorders, films.

10. That publishers should be encouraged to publish suitable educational literature, especially appropriate supplementary readers in Kiswahili and English. Incentive schemes for authors of such publications for secondary and tertiary schools and colleges should be organised.

Specific recommendations to government

It is recommended that the Ministry of Education start looking again at the question of the language media for secondary and tertiary education in the light of:

a. the growing need for 'Education for Self-Reliance' compelled by economic necessity rather than by only nationalist or humanistic considerations as was the case in the past. The economic advancement of many Tanzanians (rather than that of a tiny élite) demands that the Ministry should look again at this issue. (Otherwise, the government has a duty to tell the nation in coherent terms why it rejected the recommendations of the Makweta Commission on the issue of the medium of instruction.)

b. the growing literature on bilingualism and discourse analysis which is demonstrating that monolingual bias in the conception of one's proficiencies in languages needs to be abandoned, and that both the sociolinguistic environment beyond the school and the role of language in the development of youth culture need to be considered in choosing the medium of instruction.

It is recommended in this regard that the Ministry organise a seminar/ workshop on the question as a matter of urgency, bringing together teachers in schools, some specialists from the Institute of Education, the National Examinations Council, the University of Dar es Salaam and Sokoine University, and some educational administrators from the Ministry.

Specific recommendations to interested individuals and institutions

There is considerable evidence that individuals and institutions in Tanzania have already taken steps to implement the inevitable language media change from English to Kiswahili in a number of fields. These include those individuals and institutions which have already taken the initiative to write in or translate into Kiswahili secondary and tertiary level educational works.

1. We wish to commend these individuals and institutions and recommend that they intensify their efforts in publishing Kiswahili material on science and technology as well as other texts for the secondary and tertiary education levels. As the newly literate in adult and primary education seek to advance themselves educationally, these publications will increase their readership and become more commercially viable than they are at the moment as a result of the government's negative attitudes towards the use of Kiswahili in higher education.

2. We further recommend that the organisers of adult education programmes in the country take more individual initiatives in the direction of tapping the potential that exists for publishing more secondary and tertiary education level works in Kiswahili. Workshops could be organised for such purposes that brought together specialists from institutions like the Universities, Technical and Business Colleges and schools. Gradually the government must be compelled by the *reality* of higher education in Kiswahili to re-think its own policies in this regard.

3. Finally, it is recommended that a Language Teachers' Association should be formed by those who feel there is a great need for co-operation between teachers of Kiswahili and English in the promotion of Kiswahili as the language medium of secondary and higher education.

Note to Chapter 4

1.   This paper was written by the authors on behalf of the participants in the seminars on bilingualism held at the University of Dar es Salaam, December 1986.

References

CRIPER, C. and DODD, W.A. 1984, *Report on the Teaching of English Language and its Use as a Medium in Education in Tanzania*. Dar es Salaam: The British Council.

MLAMA, P.O. and MATTERU, M. 1978, *Haja ya Kutumia Kiswahili Kufundishia katika Elimu ya Juu*. Dar es Salaam: BAKITA.

MVUNGI, M. 1974, *Language Policy in Tanzanian Primary Schools*. MA Dissertation, University of Dar es Salaam.

RUBAGUMYA, C.M. 1986, Language planning in the Tanzanian educational system: Problems and prospects. *Journal of Multilingual and Multicultural Development*, 7, 4.

SCHMIED, J.J. 1986, English in Tanzanian education. *Bayreuth African Studies Series*, No. 5.

TRAPPES-LOMAX, H.R., BESHA, R.M. and MCHA, Y.Y. 1982, *Changing Language Media*. University of Dar es Salaam.

5 The English language support project in Tanzania

A.F. LWAITAMA and J.M. RUGEMALIRA

Background to the Project

Although the English Language Support Project was a direct result of the recommendations made by a British government-funded study (Criper & Dodd, 1984), the project arose against the background of a renewed interest in the debate about whether English could continue to function as an effective medium of education at secondary and tertiary levels. The early and mid-1970s saw heightened expectations that a change of medium was imminent. The expectations were fuelled by the expression of concern in the second Five-Year Plan (1969–74) regarding the unsatisfactory situation arising from the continued use of English as medium at secondary and tertiary levels, when a switch to Kiswahili had already been effected at primary level in 1967 (Tanzania (Government), 1969: 152). By the late 1970s there was increasing anxiety about the government's failure to fulfil the expectation (cf. the study commissioned by the National Kiswahili Council — Mlama & Matteru, 1978). Hence the renewed interest in the issue during the early 1980s.

The department of Foreign Languages and Linguistics at the University of Dar es Salaam set the pace by organising a seminar on 'The Impact on the University of the *expected* change in the medium of instruction in the Secondary Schools' in February 1980 (Trappes-Lomax, Besha & Mcha, 1982). As the then head of department, Professor Batibo, put it in the foreword, 'it was believed that this change would have a major impact on Tanzanian education, and that the task of implementing the change was likely to preoccupy educationalists for at least the *next* decade' (*ibid.* p. ii, emphasis added). Nine months after this seminar the then president, Julius Nyerere, appointed a Presidential Commission on Education to review the entire education system. The commission presented its report to the president in February 1982. Its recommendations on

36

the medium of education issue more than refuelled the expectations by actually setting a date for a change from English to Kiswahili: in January 1985 the first year of secondary school, i.e. Form I, was to start using Kiswahili (Tume ya Rais ya Elimu, 1982: 209).

Quite unexpectedly the government sought to turn the tide. In August 1983 Mr J. Makweta, who had chaired the commission and had subsequently been appointed Minister for Education, was quoted in the press (*Uhuru*, 8 August 1983) as saying that the expected change of medium was not going to take place. Apparently the Ministry of Education had published a paper in July 1984 stating the government's position *vis-à-vis* the commission's report. In the paper the government seemed to opt for the *status quo*, although its position was vaguely put: 'Both languages, English and Kiswahili, will be used as media of instruction. English will be improved at all levels of education' (Wizara ya Elimu, 1984: 19; our translation). During the same months — July/August 1984 — Criper and Dodd were carrying out the British government-funded study (henceforth Criper & Dodd Report), and it is no coincidence that their report stated that 'The Ministry of Education should issue an unambiguous circular setting out the policy on English medium education . . .' (Criper & Dodd, 1984: 73). Two months later, in October 1984, the then President Nyerere, in an unscripted speech to Swahili enthusiasts, expressed the opinion that English had to be retained as medium of instruction in order to motivate most Tanzanians to value and learn the language (*Mzalendo*, 28 October 1984). This was the first time that some light had been shed on the politics behind the rejection of the presidential commission's recommendations regarding the education media issue. The Criper & Dodd Report could thus be seen as an intervention designed to give technical respectability to the preferences of certain local political forces.

With regard to the levels of proficiency, the Criper & Dodd Report is in agreement with other studies that these levels are unsatisfactory. The latest such study, sponsored by the Canadian International Development Research Centre and conducted by two members of the University of Dar es Salaam's Foreign Languages and Linguistics department, has concluded 'that many secondary school students in Tanzania are being barred from access to knowledge as a result of the language barrier' (Roy-Campbell & Qorro, 1987: 93). 'This study, therefore, adds additional support to the call for changing the medium of instruction at secondary school level from English to Swahili' (*ibid*. p. 95). The Criper & Dodd Report does not even consider this option, but this is hardly surprising in view of the political role it was designed to fulfil. In this connection it is interesting to note that the first British Council specialist called upon to implement Criper and Dodd's recommendations, Mr M. Broughton, speculated that the government might have feared that a switch to Kiswahili would remove a formidable barrier to secondary education and would thus open the floodgates for universal secondary education, a demand the government would not be able to meet. These remarks were made at a seminar organised by the departments of Foreign Languages and Linguistics, and of Education at the University of Dar es Salaam in October 1987. Incidentally Mr Broughton left Tanzania in November 1987, that is, after having worked on the project for only eleven months.

The Project

The Criper & Dodd Report recommended the setting up of an English Language Support Project. The project would have one major objective, namely to improve the teaching and learning of English at the secondary school level. The assumption appeared to be that improvement at the secondary level would be the most cost-effective way of supporting the retention of English as medium at secondary and tertiary levels. Criper & Dodd put it thus:

> Change at the Secondary level, if, but only if, effectively carried out, will be cheaper to effect than change either at Primary level or at the multitude of post secondary institutions which exist; it is at secondary level that the most effective boost can be given to the teaching of other subjects; and it is at secondary level that the quickest effects will be felt — only four to five years.
> (Criper & Dodd, 1984: 72)

The project was conceived as a short-term programme meant to provide *support* to existing English Language Teaching (ELT) structures. It would not directly concern itself with the development of syllabi and course-books, and no new local administrative posts were going to be created. Indeed, the current project co-ordinator, Mr I. Pearson, remarked, at a seminar organised by the University of Dar es Salaam's Foreign Languages and Linguistics department (August 1988) that there was no need for local counterparts to the British Council English Language officers currently running the project. In short, the project aimed at resuscitating the ELT system and then leaving it to manage as best it could at the end of the short project period.

In view of the foregoing it is not surprising that the project concentrates on one 'specific area of implementation' — a reading improvement programme. The assumption here might be that improvement in reading skills would raise students' vocabulary, and in this way enhance the viability of English medium education. The programme is seen as a means of creating, in the classroom, 'meaning-focused input' (Dr Rod Ellis, personal communication) which will lead to students' spontaneous use of English.

The project's total budget is in the region £2 million spanning a period of four years. It covers costs for employing up to ten Specialist English Language officers (KELTs), 30 short-term scholarships each year for study in Britain, book donations, and tours by ELT specialists from Britain. At the time of writing, nine of the KELT posts have already been filled. Seven of these are stationed in the seven zones that have been established for the purpose. One is based in the department of Education at the University of Dar es Salaam, and the other is the overall co-ordinator of the project.

The book presentation programme consists of a set of graded class readers, class library texts, reading cards, and a course-book. Except for the last item the bulk of the graded class readers and library texts were purchased from the Institute for Applied Language Studies at the University of Edinburgh, where one of the authors of the report works. The course-book — the *English in Use* series (Grant & Wang'ombe, 1979) — was initially developed for Kenyan schools and limited copies have been brought in, presumably as a temporary measure, to fill the felt need for a course-book to accompany the readers. The books are donated to schools 'year by year, sequentially, from Form I to Form IV' (Criper & Dodd, 1984: 77–8). A limit of 234 schools with which the project is involved has been established (J.G. Tetlow, personal communication); 105 of these are central government schools run by the Ministry of Education while the rest are run by a variety of religious denominations and other agencies.

Three-month scholarships are awarded each year to 30 secondary school teachers selected jointly by the KELT team and the Ministry of Education. They attend specially designed courses at Leeds University and Plymouth college in Britain. In turn a number of ELT specialists from Britain are invited to make short visits to Tanzania largely to provide an evaluative input into the project implementation process as well as to contribute to the seminars for teachers of English. Provision has been made for such seminars to be jointly organised by the Ministry of Education and the project's KELT team (each member of the team has a landrover for the purpose). The seminars are meant to introduce the teachers to the mechanics of administering the reading programme.

To conclude this section on the project, it is worth noting that two recommendations of the Criper & Dodd Report do not appear to have been adopted. These are a six-month English conversion course for students entering secondary schools, and a compulsory English language course for Forms V and VI. It would appear that these were seen as requiring major financial and administrative commitments on the part of the British Overseas Development Administration and the Tanzanian Ministry of Education.

Interim Evaluation and Conclusion

At the time of writing (September 1988) the project is in its second year, having started two years behind schedule. It may thus be too early to make any conclusive evaluation of the project. However, some interim observations can be made.

First, certain components of the project are bound to have a positive impact on the teaching and learning of English in Tanzania. The book donations, the short-term courses for teachers in Britain, the refresher seminars, and any locally developed materials that may be produced as part of the project, add to the pool of resources potentially available to ELT endeavours in Tanzania, now and in the future. But the cultural appropriateness of some of the books could be questioned from the standpoint of the official socialist ideology. This is especially true of some of the Forms I and II readers which were initially produced for countries whose ideology is capitalist. Books in this category include *In the Beginning* by J. Christopher, *The Magic Garden* and *Fast Money* by K.R. Cripwell.

Interestingly, for Forms III and IV, it was decided to order abridged and simplified editions (where these are available) of the books which have been on the reading programme for the past 15 years. This development is interesting because there were people on the KELT team who would have liked to see these books replaced. They were unhappy with the politically slanted themes under which the books were taught as well as the level of difficulty of most of these texts. Perhaps the decision to retain the same books was made in the light of the broader principles of the project which excluded any major structural changes.

Secondly, the project's basic objective of contributing to better teaching and learning of English in Tanzania is laudable. Although some people might question the strategy adopted, namely a reading improvement programme, we actually believe that this is the right strategy, especially when a switch to Kiswahili medium in education is seen as inevitable.

Without doubt, when such a switch has been effected, English will retain a very important role in the education system as a 'library language' (Trappes-Lomax *et al.*, 1982: 29). In a situation where English is not the language in which students write, listen or speak, but only read, a reading improvement programme seems to be the most cost-effective strategy to adopt.

However, it is unfortunate that this project was, from its very conception in the Criper & Dodd Report (p. 73), tied to the continued use of English as medium in secondary schools. As such the project runs the risk of appearing to be hostile to the development of Kiswahili as at least another language of higher education. This situation might complicate future assessment of the project. Should the project fail to reinstate English as the only medium of education at secondary and tertiary levels, then other positive aspects of the project might be overshadowed.

Finally, future generations of Tanzanians may assess the project as having provided the excuse for not taking the difficult decision to organise for the inevitable change of media. In the meantime the debate about whether the time is now ripe for Kiswahili to replace English as the main medium of education at secondary and tertiary levels continues.

References

CHRISTOPHER, J. 1972, *In The Beginning*. Essex: Longmans.

CRIPER, C. and DODD, W.A. 1984, *Report on the Teaching of the English Language and its Use as a Medium in Education in Tanzania*. Dar es Salaam: The British Council.

CRIPWELL, K.R. 1977, *The Magic Garden*. London: Collins.

— 1978, *Fast Money*. Glasgow: Collins.

GRANT, N.J.H. and WANG'OMBE, C.R. 1979, *English in Use*. Essex: Longman (Books 1–4).

MLAMA, P.O. and MATTERU, M. 1978, *Haja ya Kutumia Kiswahili Kufundishia katika Elimu ya Juu*. Dar es Salaam: BAKITA.

ROY-CAMPBELL, Z.M. and QORRO, M.P. 1987, *A Survey of the Reading Competence in English of Secondary School Students in Tanzania*. University of Dar es Salaam.

TANZANIA (Government) 1969, *The Second Five-Year Plan for Economic and Social Development 1969–1974. Volume I, General Analysis*. Dar es Salaam.

TRAPPES-LOMAX, H.R., BESHA, R.M. and MCHA, Y.Y. 1982, *Changing Language Media*. University of Dar es Salaam.

TUME YA RAIS YA ELIMU 1982, *Mfumo wa Elimu ya Tanzania 1981–2000, Juzuu la Kwanza*. Dar es Salaam.

WIZARA YA ELIMU 1984, *Mfumo wa Elimu Tanzania: Maamuzi ya Chama na Serikali kuhusu Ripoti ya Tume ya Raisi ya Elimu ya 1982*. Dar es Salaam.

6 When international languages clash: The possible detrimental effects on development of the conflict between English and Kiswahili in Tanzania

S. YAHYA-OTHMAN

> That Tanzanian education is bilingual is . . . neither to be wondered at nor regretted. But the particular nature of this bilingualism, and its implications for the learning individual and for the developing society, are not likewise to be accepted without question. (Trappes-Lomax & Besha, 1982)

Introduction

The purpose of this chapter is to examine 'the implications for the learning individual' of Tanzania's bilingualism, and further, to question the nature of this bilingualism. That nature has been admirably discussed by Trappes-Lomax and Besha, and by various other writers. If I touch on it, it will be but briefly.

I am making two assumptions: first, that Kiswahili is generally accepted to be an international language; second, that there is broad agreement that Kiswahili in Tanzania is not in blissful co-existence with its partner, English. On the first assumption, it need only be said that if an international language is one which is spoken beyond the borders of its native land, by speakers additional to its native speakers, then Kiswahili qualifies eminently. It may have several 'native lands', but its distribution is no longer confined to these lands, nor to its native speakers. It is being taught in universities and other centres throughout the world, and is being used by speakers of various nationalities to communicate with each other, and with native speakers. Where it differs from English, then, is in the extent and density of its distribution. The second assumption, too, has been shown to underlie arguments by several writers: Criper & Dodd (1984), Lwaitama *et al.* (this volume), Mlama & Matteru (1978), Rugemalira *et al.* (this volume), Rubagumya (1986), Trappes-Lomax (this volume), among others. It is the stress and strains which manifest themselves in such arguments that constitute the theme of this chapter. This second assumption still needs to be justified, although it may appear to many absurd that such a need should exist.

Language and Development

It may seem axiomatic to state that language is an essential ingredient in the development process. The demands of modernisation are such that they must involve the dissemination of the various modernising agents both among different classes in the society and within different fields of interest. The modernising process is a process of conflict: conflict between tradition and innovation, between social mobilisation and social differentiation, between mass tendencies and individual specialisation (Eisenstadt, 1966). No wonder, then, that protest and violent eruptions are sometimes a direct consequence of this process. This conflict may, on the one hand, be mitigated by the language used in the society — appeals made in the developing countries on the use of a national language in order to foster greater unity have recently become more insistent. On the other hand, the conflict itself may actually be *fostered* by the languages spoken in the community and the differing allegiances associated with them. Examples of disharmony in society arising directly from linguistic differences are legion.

Whatever the role played by language in the development process, that role cannot be over-emphasised: the recognition that education is a necessary prerequisite for development is long-established (Bailey, 1972). Education is seen to be crucial to developmental change. It constitutes the start of the development process for the individual, and by extension, for the society. Education, both formal and informal, is carried out largely through the medium of some language, although this medium may be accompanied by other less conventionalised and more implicit modes. Ongoing debates in various countries on the choice of medium are a reflection of the significance of language in the educational process. The movement for the use of the mother tongue in primary education (Bull, 1964), the movement for immersion programmes (Swain & Lapkin, 1982), the concern of parents that their children should be proficient in the relevant foreign language, are all consequences of the overwhelming importance attached to language in education. Indeed, the proposition that children learn best only when they are highly proficient in the medium of instruction has never been disputed.

There are two aspects relating to language in its developmental role that seem relevant to this discussion. First, the individual may change in the course of his life from being a receiver of education, a learner, to becoming a dispenser of education, a teacher (Bailey, 1972). These two situations in the life of the individual may correlate with different kinds of language proficiency. In the former case, the individual needs to be able to *understand* and *interpret* what is communicated to him, and here, a receptive competence may be sufficient. In the latter case, the individual needs to be able to disseminate the knowledge that he has acquired in such a way that others can understand *him*. He would then need a productive competence. Matters may be complicated by the fact that the language of acquisition of new knowledge may not necessarily be identical to the language of transmission of that knowledge.

Secondly, in most developing countries, since educational opportunities are restricted, those who manage to receive a reasonable amount of education come to constitute a class of 'opinion leaders', mediators between new knowledge and the vast majority of the population (Brandt, 1972). Such opinion leaders, by virtue of their education, acquire, or are assumed to have, influence and 'a voice'. They can consequently decide on and adapt the information that is passed on, either to suit their own purposes, or to make it, in *their* consideration, more 'accessible' to their audience. Communication is thus a variable of overwhelming significance for those on the receiving end. The language competence possessed by the opinion leaders would inevitably affect the quality of information that is passed on to the majority.

All these issues are relevant in the consideration of the position of the languages in Tanzania in relation to their statuses as media or vehicles of education, and, in turn, of development. I shall turn to this after a brief consideration of the situation in Africa generally.

Language and Development in Africa

The 'opinion leaders' in Africa gain their influence and power not only through the fact of their education, but also, because of that, through their control of several languages in what is invariably a multilingual situation, in which the languages of wider communication are acquired only through the higher education system, and are therefore, by necessity, accessible only to a minority. It has been noted that multilingualism is for the most part the preserve of Third World countries (Todd, 1984). Africa is the epitome of both underdevelopment and multilingualism. With over a thousand vernacular languages spoken south of the Sahara, the complexity of the African linguistic situation hardly needs emphasising (Denny, 1963). These two phenomena, Africa's underdevelopment and her multilingualism might have had no connection historically, but at present there are indications that some of the language policies adopted by some African countries can be justified in terms of Africa's underdevelopment.

In both anglophone and francophone countries governments have largely adopted the policy of teaching English or French in primary school and making pupils use it in secondary school. In other words, in primary school pupils follow their lessons in one of the vernacular languages while learning English or French as a subject, and then switch over to these second languages in the later primary years or in secondary school. One reason for this state is of course political: governments cannot risk the upheaval that might be precipitated by the choice of one or a few vernaculars for use in the whole educational system. But another equally important reason is economic. Even if it were possible to choose some vernacular language, the resources are not available to train teachers, develop grammars and orthographies, produce and translate texts, for the vernacular languages. The consequence of this is that no African country south of the Sahara has so far used an African language as a medium of instruction in secondary and higher education. Tanzania may soon become an exception to this pattern (see the following section), but even here, the hesitation of the last two decades can be explained in part by the lack of resources.

The pedagogical problems that arise from these policies vary only in degree — they are otherwise the same. In the francophone countries, French is introduced earlier than English is in those countries where it is used. Also, in some of the latter countries, such as Cameroon, the only medium of instruction is English (Todd, 1984). But in all cases, the pupils are receiving education in a language which is at best a second language, and at worst a foreign language. They learn a language which they do not use, except in the classroom. The teachers are themselves poorly trained and poorly equipped. The resources for the expansion of the language curricula are not available (Criper & Dodd, 1984; Denny, 1963; Fawcett,

1970; Gorman, 1970; Perren, 1969; Todd, 1984; Trappes-Lomax, this volume). The result is that pupils enter secondary school with hardly an adequate knowledge of the medium of instruction to enable their teachers to educate them properly. Thus the development of all these countries is ultimately adversely affected, since the products of such educational systems are individuals who have been hampered by linguistic deficiencies in their thinking, in their critical observation, in their questioning of ideas and facts, and in their interpretation of what is communicated to them. The fact that they continue to pass examinations is hardly evidence of their ability to contribute fully to the development of their countries.

It is in reaction to this situation that there is pressure now, at least in those countries where the political consequences are not envisaged to be catastrophic, to urge the greater use of the vernacular of indigenous languages in the education system. In the case of Namibia, for example, there are attempts to forestall the problems occasioned by the linguistic policies of other African countries before Namibia gets its independence. Since one of the languages of wider communication, Afrikaans, arouses very strong negative attitudes, and the other, English, is also related to the colonial domination of Namibians at a time of high political consciousness, the atmosphere may be right in that context for the acceptance and development of some of the vernaculars in higher education (Phillipson, Skutnabb-Kangas & Africa, 1986). The policy of Swapo, however, is to follow the traditional path of using the vernaculars for primary education, and accept English as a national language and medium for higher education. In the case of Tanzania, one of the indigenous languages, Kiswahili, has historically come to acquire a neutral, non-ethnic position, as we shall see in the next section of this chapter.

The Tanzanian Situation

In relation to media of education, the Tanzanian situation has been well described (Criper & Dodd, 1984; Lwaitama *et al.* (this volume), Mlama & Matteru, 1978; Mohammed, 1975; Mvungi, 1974; Polomé & Hill, 1980; Trappes-Lomax, this volume; among others), but it may still bear further mention in a summarised form.

Tanzanian children receive seven years of primary education in the medium of Kiswahili, which is not the mother tongue of all, but the second language of most (an estimated 90% in 1971; Abdulaziz, 1971), and the one indigenous language which has been widely developed and has received the status of national language. These children begin learning English in the third year of primary school, for about four hours per week. Following primary education, for the small minority (2.7% in 1981) who manage to enter secondary school, there is a sudden and almost complete switch in the medium of teaching to English. All subjects, with the exception of Kiswahili and Siasa (political education), are at this time supposed to be taught in English.

The status of English itself has in recent years changed from second language to foreign language. This shift has been succinctly covered by Trappes-Lomax (this volume), who notes that the functions normally associated with a second language have become virtually extinct for English in Tanzania, and the only one that remains is that of medium of secondary and higher education. Rugemalira *et al.* (this volume) emphasise this point by saying:

> English is not the language used to address the bus conductor, to enquire about a balance at the bank, to ask for stamps at the post office, to reserve a seat at the railway station, to speak to the medical assistant at the health centre, to buy an allocation of 'essential commodities' at the 'Kaya' shop, or to make a statement at the police station. Nor is English the language spoken by Members of Parliament while debating a bill.

What this means is that English has ceased to be *used* for day to day communication, except in communication with foreigners. It is essentially a classroom language, and more restrictedly each day, a language for writing reports in government and parastatal organisations.

Now, it may be argued that the switch in medium in itself is not necessarily a negative or harmful event. Most colonial education in Tanzania was conducted through such a switch, though it may have come earlier. The products of that education system are the people at present making decisions about the education of the new generations. While that education system may not have been relevant or efficient or successful in terms of Tanzania's present goals, it was effective in terms of the goals of the colonialists — pupils learned what they were taught, they were educated, the few of them, to the highest levels both in Tanzania and abroad. Moreover, at a more general level, the recommendations made by UNESCO in relation to the use of vernacular languages in education took account of the possibility, where the vernacular is not a national language, of a switch from the vernacular to the national language later in the education process (UNESCO, 1953). The switch, therefore, is not necessarily evil.

But what has happened in Tanzania is that the switch is now taking place amid a totally different set of circumstances from that holding in colonial times. Three of these circumstances are particularly pertinent:

a. The status of Kiswahili — this has risen steadily since independence. Kiswahili has changed from being a 'vernacular' language to being a national language, to being an international language. Its ability to be a vehicle of development is constantly enhanced. It is the language by which the masses of Tanzanians communicate and are communicated with, and effectively by which government is run. The ascending status of Kiswahili has inevitably resulted in a corresponding decline in the status of English, touched on above.

b. The attitudes of Tanzanians — partly arising from (a), the attitudes of all sections of society towards the two major languages have changed considerably (Rubagumya, 1986). Because the spheres of communication for Kiswahili have widened, it has assumed a privileged position. Conversely, English has fallen from its social pedestal, and come to be considered more as the language of foreigners and *'wasomi'* (intellectuals), irrelevant to the needs of the ordinary people.

c. The economic situation — the vicious spiral which gives rise to a causal chain between the economy and the provision of services has not failed to affect the teaching of languages. That the Tanzanian standards of English have fallen has been said so many times and by so many people that it now sounds like a bad comedy line. Only it is not a joke. The lack of trained teachers, teaching materials, material incentives for the profession, contributed to a situation where very little English is being taught, and very little is taught in it. This situation is well documented. At any particular level in secondary and higher education, only a small percentage could be said to possess a level of English necessary for them to follow their particular studies.

These three circumstances are obviously interdependent, and all have directly given rise to the present situation, in which a sudden switch in medium may be viewed as negative and retrograde. I now look more closely at the consequences of this situation.

Consequences

The consequences of the language policy being followed by Tanzania at present are perhaps implied in the discussion above. I shall try to present them in a more explicit manner, and also to show the interconnections between them.

Following from the circumstances discussed above, the performance of students in English has fallen appallingly. Of the 2,419 pupils tested by Criper and Dodd at all levels of the educational system, only 29% of the total had attained a level for easily following studies at their respective levels (Criper & Dodd, 1984); in 1986, nearly 50% of Form IV leavers scored F in English (National Examinations Council, 1986); in 1987, 15% of university entrants scored under 50% in the University Screening Test conducted by the Communication Skills Unit (CSU). Consequently, the medium in the secondary schools is effectively a mixture of English and Kiswahili. This was noted by Mlama & Matteru (1978) and also by Mohammed (1975). Students do not learn when the subject is presented in English; the teacher himself may not have sufficient proficiency to present that subject matter in English. A switch to Kiswahili therefore achieves the immediate communication and learning needs, but does not liberate the students from assignment and examination requirements in English. In the same CSE examination mentioned above, it is noteworthy that those students who obtained a fourth-division pass (requiring a pass in at least one subject), most commonly show a pass grade in either Kiswahili or Siasa, the two subjects taught in the Kiswahili medium. Above the secondary level, it has also been found necessary to introduce special 'remedial' courses prior to University training. The Communication Skills Unit (CSU) of the University of Dar es Salaam is approaching its tenth year doing that job. The medical faculty has since last year been providing crash courses not only in English but in other subjects for its new entrants, prior to their medical courses.

The continued insistence on the use of English at the higher levels has meant that students do not have sufficient time to devote to the conscious use of new Kiswahili terms. Basic concepts relating to, for instance, mathematics, the sciences, the sociocultural context, start to be developed in the Kiswahili medium, but then have to be extended in the new medium. At a stage when the pupils' cognitive processes are at their developmental peak, they use not Kiswahili but English. However, outside the classroom, they have to discourse in Kiswahili. But they have neither the terminology nor the skill to do this in Kiswahili in relation to their *educational* subjects. The result is that, as Mkude (1982: 61) observes: 'Any attempt to use Kiswahili as an educational tool at this [University] level now would constitute a major leap upward since it would skip the intermediate stage. In practice this would mean grafting a tertiary level of experience onto a primary level of literacy.'

This restricted use of Kiswahili in the educational field means that the development of Kiswahili is thwarted in various respects. The use of a language as medium gives it an additional function which allows it to expand. There is normally a two-way feedback in the use of language — the medium input grows on the wide communication input and *vice versa*, so that each sphere gains enrichment from the other. The classroom use of the language meets largely ideational needs — the dissemination of information and ideas; the outside use meets largely interpersonal needs — the pupil relating to and establishing contact with peers, family and friends (Halliday, 1973). But strictly the two functions are inseparable. And yet in the Tanzanian case an artificial barrier has been created, Kiswahili being used largely for the latter function, English for the former.

Over the years, since the founding of the Inter-territorial Language Committee in 1930, there have been vigorous attempts to standardise Kiswahili, and to develop terminology which would facilitate its role as a vehicle for modernisation. BAKITA (The National Swahili Council) has developed various sets of terminology for secondary schools; a range of books have been translated from English for the higher levels; more recently, an international committee has developed working terminology for Biology, Chemistry, Physics and Linguistics which can be used up to University level. But the development of new terminology must include its dissemination, to allow for feedback on its efficacy and relevance from its eventual users, the students in schools and universities. This is not at the moment possible (and it needs to be said in fairness that it is impossible not only in Tanzania but in the other Kiswahili-speaking countries as well). The schools and universities do not officially use Kiswahili as medium, and there is consequently no provision for the trial use of these new items. The result is a stalemate. The teaching and social situations which are necessary for the practice and acceptance of new terms are non-existent; all the same, researchers are expected to continue their search for new terminology and their work of translation. But, not surprisingly, they become frustrated when their work has to wait for some distant decision at some unknown date by some indeterminable person or institution. This situation feeds on that discussed above, in that the lack of opportunities for the introduction of new terminology affects the communicative competence not only of individual students, but of entire educational generations.

This may have the consequence that the conceptualisation abilities of the precious few who receive higher education become stunted. It has been noted that conceptualisation is an essential function of language for the individual (Le Page, 1964). In school, the student must be allowed not only to learn his various subjects, but also to think about those subjects and others, and to demonstrate the results of his thinking. The Tanzanian student, I suggest, is in the process of losing this function. His problem is not just that his Kiswahili conceptualisation abilities are nipped at an early stage, but that these abilities are not allowed to develop much in English either. The student's cognitive development comes to rest on a weak and unstable foundation of Kiswahili/English 'labels' for concepts which are but vaguely grasped. Instead of the language of education becoming a liberating, door-opening agent, it (or they) becomes constricting and restricting factors. Basic concepts which should grow with a child, and be added to constantly as the child learns more, are shaken midway by an ineffective change in medium.

I would argue, therefore, that the developmental process in Tanzania may be deeply disturbed by the conflicting attempts of its two major international languages to exert influence over the same area — the educational field. In particular, the functions of conceptualisation and communication are being served by neither language. Tanzanians' ability to think in innovative ways, to apply such thinking in the development of new ideas which may effect changes in their societies, to bring about modernisation, is being threatened. Secondly, their ability to make more widely known those ideas which they do manage to develop, to pass on what they learn, is being reduced. The consequences will come to visit the entire society.

Conclusion

The arguments presented in this chapter have not been based on any empirical research, but on an intuitive understanding and interested observation of Tanzania's educational system and the ways the products of that system affect and are affected by society.

The argument is not that it is impossible or even difficult to develop under the conditions of two international languages operating in the schools — examples such as those of Canada and Switzerland would immediately quash such an argument; nor is the argument that it is impossible to develop with a foreign language as the medium of instruction — all the former colonies are doing precisely that, and their attendant problems do not all have to be laid at the language door. The argument is that it would be extremely difficult to modernise with English as medium under the *present socio-economic conditions in Tanzania*. And the most crucial of these conditions is the continued equivocation relating to the switch in medium. For almost 20 years Tanzanians have known that a shift in medium is forthcoming, but they have not known when; they have known that the government has singularly failed to implement its own policy, but they have not known why; they have been persuaded that English needs to remain the medium of instruction, but they have yet to receive a reasonable justification. The consequence is that, on the one hand, any attempts to raise the standards of English are met with the response 'What for?' (Note the recent dismissive reaction of 'concerned linguists and educationalists', most of them teachers of English, to the Criper/Dodd proposals on the improvement of English (Rugemalira *et al.*, this volume).) On the other hand, attempts to improve and develop the standards of Kiswahili are denied official sanction in the higher educational fields for use and validation. This stalemate is what causes concern.

Tanzania has long been held up as an enviable example of effective and smooth language planning (Abdulaziz, 1971; Khamis, 1974; Mlama & Mvungi, 1982; Polomé & Hill, 1980; Whiteley, 1969). In relation to Kiswahili vs. the vernaculars, the government has acted decisively and early to effect a situation which is recognised to be in the best interests of all. It is therefore surprising that the same government seems to be gripped with indecisiveness in relation to Kiswahili vs. English. The policy has been set out, but the implementation is not forthcoming. One can only hope that the educational system will not have suffered irreversibly by the time, in what future nobody knows, the decision is made to 'make official' the use of Kiswahili as medium.

References

ABDULAZIZ, M.H. 1971, Tanzania's national language policy and the rise of Swahili political culture. In W.H. WHITELEY (ed.) *Language Use and Social Change*. London: Oxford University Press.

BAILEY, W.C. 1972, The role of education in bringing about change. In J.B. ACEVES (ed.) *Aspects of Cultural Change*. Athens: Southern Anthropological Society.

BRANDT, E.A. 1972, Language, linguistics and social change: Retrospect and prospect. In J.B. ACEVES (ed.) *Aspects of Cultural Change*. Athens: Southern Anthropological Society.

BULL, W. 1964, The use of vernacular languages in fundamental education. In D. HYMES (ed.) *Language in Culture and Society*. New York: Harper and Row.

CRIPER, C. and DODD, W.A. 1984, *Report on the Teaching of English Language and its Use as a Medium in Education in Tanzania*. Dar es Salaam: The British Council.

DENNY, N. 1963, Languages and education in Africa. In J. SPENCER (ed.) *Language in Africa*. Cambridge: Cambridge University Press.

EISENSTADT, S.N. 1966, *Modernisation: Protest and Change*. Englewood Cliffs, NJ: Prentice-Hall.

FAWCETT, R.P. 1970, The medium of education in the lower primary school in Africa with special reference to Kenya. In T.P. GORMAN (ed.) *Language in Education in Eastern Africa*. Nairobi: Oxford University Press.

GORMAN, T.P. 1970, Introduction: Educational implications of multilingualism in Eastern Africa. In T.P. GORMAN (ed.) *Language in Education in Eastern Africa*. Nairobi: Oxford University Press.

HALLIDAY, M.A.K. 1973, *Explorations in the Functions of Language*. London: Edward Arnold.

KHAMIS, A.M. 1974, Swahili as a national language. In G. RUHUMBIKA (ed.) *Towards Ujamaa*. Dar es Salaam: East African Literature Bureau.

LE PAGE, R. 1964, *The National Language Question*. London: Oxford University Press.

MKUDE, D.J. 1982, Matching education with communicative skills in Kiswahili. In H.R. TRAPPES-LOMAX, R.M. BESHA and Y.Y. MCHA (eds) *Changing Language Media*. University of Dar es Salaam.

MLAMA, P.O. and MATTERU, M.L. 1978, *Haja ya kutumia Kiswahili kufundishia katika elimu ya juu*. Dar es Salaam: Baraza la Kiswahili la Taifa.

MLAMA, P.O. and MVUNGI, M. 1982, Past language policy and research in educational practice in Tanzania. In H.R. TRAPPES-LOMAX, R.M. BESHA and Y.Y. MCHA (eds) *Changing Language Media*. University of Dar es Salaam.

MOHAMMED, M.A. 1975, *The Introduction of Kiswahili as a Medium of Instruction in Tanzania Secondary Schools: A Diagnostic and Evaluative Study*. MA dissertation, University of Dar es Salaam.

MVUNGI, M. 1974, *Language Policy in Tanzania Primary Schools with Emphasis on Implementation*. MA dissertation, University of Dar es Salaam.

NATIONAL EXAMINATIONS COUNCIL 1986, *Results of the Certificate of Secondary Education Examination*. Dar es Salaam: National Examinations Council.

PHILLIPSON, R., SKUTNABB-KANGAS, T. and AFRICA, H. 1986, Namibian educational language planning: English for liberation or neo-colonialism? In B. SPOLSKY (ed.) *Language in Education in Multilingual Settings*. Clevedon, Avon: Multilingual Matters.

POLOMÉ, E.C. and HILL, C.P. (eds) 1980, *Language in Tanzania*. London: Oxford University Press.

RUBAGUMYA, C.M. 1986, Language planning in the Tanzania educational system: problems and prospects. *Journal of Multilingual and Multicultural Development* 7, 4, 283–300.

SWAIN, M. and LAPKIN, S. 1982, *Evaluating Bilingual Education: A Canadian Case Study*. Clevedon, Avon: Multilingual Matters.

TODD, G.E. 1984, Language options for education in a multilingual society: Cameroon. In C. KENNEDY (ed.) *Language Planning and Language Education*. London: George Allen and Unwin.

TRAPPES-LOMAX, H.R. and BESHA, R.M. 1982, Educational bilingualism — theory and practice. In H.R. TRAPPES-LOMAX, R.M. BESHA and Y.Y. MCHA (eds) *Changing Language Media*. University of Dar es Salaam.

TRAPPES-LOMAX, H.R., BESHA, R.M. and MCHA, Y.Y. (eds) 1982, *Changing Language Media*. Papers from the seminar 'The impact on the University of the expected change in the medium of instruction in the secondary schools'. University of Dar es Salaam.

UNESCO 1953, The use of vernacular languages in education. Monographs on fundamental education, No. 8. Paris: UNESCO.

WHITELEY, W.H. 1969, *Swahili: The Rise of a National Language*. London: Methuen.

7 English language teaching and learning in Tanzanian primary schools

H.M. BATIBO

Introduction

That the standard of English language teaching and learning has gone down in our primary schools is a generally accepted claim. However, English language specialists are at variance when it comes to pinpointing the crucial factor or factors which have brought about this decline. The need to identify the major reasons behind this fall in the English language performance and standards in primary schools prompted the Ministry of Education in 1982 to appoint a team to investigate this problem. The writer was asked to lead the team.

The following are therefore the writer's personal findings and impressions on the problem arrived at (i) after a systematic analysis of the data obtained in one region in which he carried out his investigations; (ii) following discussions of the findings with English language experts and teachers at the University of Dar es Salaam; (iii) after consulting reports and studies on the same or related subjects carried out in Tanzania, and other regions in Africa. The discussions in this chapter are personal views and have nothing to do with the final report of the team appointed by the Ministry. This chapter aims at examining the main factors which have contributed to the decline in English language in our primary schools and at suggesting some ways of dealing with the situation.

General Working Atmosphere in Primary Schools

After visiting and observing classes in a number of urban and rural

54

areas during part of May 1982, the writer was able to identify three types of primary schools.

(a) Urban primary schools

These are primary schools found in urban settings. Such schools are normally well equipped and have a number of good facilities including furniture, several books, good buildings and surroundings. The majority of teachers are ex-Form IV or long-service class VIII teachers. Most of them are ladies, usually wives of civil servants. Pupils are generally knowledge-able, well motivated and may have various reasons for learning English. Both the school and the environment would motivate them. My short research revealed that a good number of the urban primary school pupils expressed interest in English language because of their desire to understand what was said in films, radio and newspapers.

(b) Long-established rural primary schools

These are primary schools which have been in existence prior to the UPE (Universal Primary Education) programme in 1977. Such schools are normally adequately equipped. They have the basic facilities such as desks, blackboards and satisfactory buildings. The teachers are usually Grade C (primary school leaver) with a few Grade A (secondary school leaver). Normally the headteacher is a Grade A. The pupils are relatively less active and may have little motivation for learning English, although some facilities would be readily available to teach it more or less adequately. Both the school and the surrounding would not normally provide a good incentive to learn English.

(c) The newly established rural primary schools

These are primary schools which were largely established after the UPE crash programme in 1977. Such schools are usually inadequately equipped. Many of the buildings may have unfinished roofs, windows, doors, etc. Some may not even have desks so that big stones or concrete blocks are used instead. Some of them may not have permanent blackboards or writing facilities like chalk, copybooks, pencils, etc. In many cases, the teachers are semi-qualified and are far fewer than the number of streams in the schools. The motivation of the pupils to learn the English language would be nearly non-existent. To them English is as remote as the name England is in their minds. During my investigations, most of the negative or blank answers about English language came from such schools. Many pupils remained silent when asked if they liked English or why they liked it.

The Position of English Language Teaching and Learning in General

On analysing the data obtained after interviews with primary school pupils, teachers, headteachers, tutors in Colleges of National Education, education officials and language experts, and after studying the earlier reports and researches on the subject, the writer listed the main causes of the decline in the standard of English as follows.

(a) Lack of textbooks, reference books and subsidiary reading materials

After visiting a number of urban and rural primary schools, the author found that most of these schools lacked textbooks, reference books and subsidiary reading materials. The situation was as follows.

(i) Textbooks

The general position regarding textbooks is set out in Table 7.1.

TABLE 7.1

Name of textbook	% of schools using it	Average of pupils per book
English for Tanzanian Schools (Ministry of Education)	71	8.5
Communicative English for Tanzania (Ministry of Education)	6	Only teacher's book
Primary English for Tanzania (Ministry of Education)	11	Only teacher's book
New Oxford English Course (F.G. French)	6	Only teacher's book
Modern English (Neil Osman)	6	Only teacher's book

(ii) Reference and subsidiary books

The majority of primary schools, especially those in the rural areas, did not have any reference or subsidiary books at all. The few English books found in some of the schools were, in most cases, dilapidated and often in small numbers. Only one school had a series of recently published short stories. This problem has been mentioned in a number of reports, e.g. Ezekiel (1978), Jarvis (1979), Tume ya Rais ya Elimu (1982). Most teachers mentioned it as problem No. 1. The lack of books has, in fact, created the following problems:

— lack of visual conceptualisation and memorisation of structures and vocabulary,
— lack of support when reading or repeating sentences,
— difficulty in concentration,
— difficulty in making individual revision and reference,
— difficulty in practising or reinforcing what had been learnt,
— difficulty in creating reading habits in English,
— difficulty in motivating pupils without visual aids to attract their attention, especially in the lower classes.

Up to very recently, the only textbook which was found in most primary schools was *English for Tanzanian Schools* (*ETS*). However, as mentioned by Ezekiel (1978), this textbook, like many others, was not so useful because its passages were too long; the level of difficulty was in many cases too high; most of the lessons planned to cover 30 or 40 minutes needed more time; the books lacked enough exercises for pupils; there was lack of other materials such as charts to accompany some of the books; there was lack of sequential progression from one book to another; and there was a shortage of books for particular classes in several schools.

The problem of textbooks and reference books was even more acute in the newly built UPE schools where even teachers did not have proper English book guides, textbooks or reference books. Although the Minister of Education in her budget speech for the 1982/83 fiscal year stated that the sharing of textbooks had been reduced from ten to five pupils to a book, in several rural schools the fact remained that there were no English language books except for isolated cases of one or two *ETS* textbooks or some of the old Oxford Concise Grammar books which do not constitute complete series.

This is indeed a significant regression especially when it is remembered that in the past, middle schools or upper primary schools had enough textbooks for each pupil and there were even mini-libraries from which pupils could borrow books for personal reference and reading. This is indeed still the case in some private primary schools, like the Stockley Primary School in Dodoma which the writer visited, where they have a variety of textbooks and reading materials in English on various subjects. This helps in training the pupils on a variety of subjects and themes in English.

(b) Lack of competence on the part of the teachers

The lack of competent teachers who teach English was rated as problem No. 2, not only from the research findings but also after several interviews with the teachers themselves and tutors in the Colleges of National Education. The significance of this problem was also highlighted in Katigula (1976), Jarvis (1979) and Tume ya Rais ya Elimu (1982).

There are three aspects to the problem:

(i) Poor command of the English language

Many of the English language teachers at primary school level are not adequately proficient in the language. This includes Form IV leavers. During my investigations, less than one third of the teachers impressed me as people with adequate proficiency in the language. Most of the others, especially the UPE and the recent Grade C teachers, made many inexcusable mistakes in grammar and pronunciation. The following are typical of some of the errors the writer recorded:

1. 'Have he got a car?'
2. 'He accepted them grateful.'
3. 'These stamps have on letters and sent through the post.'
4. 'Look the sentence in the blackboard.'
5. 'Stand all greet the visitors.'

Also, many teachers failed to pronounce the sounds /θ/, /ð/, /ɪ/, /ʊ/; they used the sounds /s/, /z/, /i/ and /u/ instead. This resulted in confusion where minimal pairs like *thin/sin, both/boss, sick/seek, bit/beat* were in the same text. This poor command of the language must have contributed to the lack of interest or confidence in the language for some of them. They taught it only because they had to.

(ii) Inappropriate methodology

The writer's own observations of the primary school teachers and his discussions with the tutors in a number of Colleges of National Education revealed that most of the primary school teachers were half-baked in terms of training in English language teaching methodology. Although the majority had spent up to two years at a Teachers' College, they could not devise their own teaching strategies and materials to fit the conditions they found in their schools. As a result, they depended very heavily on textbooks. Since the textbooks themselves were inadequate, their performance in teaching left a lot to be desired. The situation was even more difficult with the UPE teachers who, in most cases, taught in schools which were under-equipped.

As a result, many of the teachers resorted to translation methods from Kiswahili or to obliging the pupils to chant together structures or sentences which had been listed on the blackboard. In this case, the teacher did not bother to correct individual mistakes, which went undetected, nor to ensure that the pupils understood what they were chanting. The problem of lack of confidence in the teaching methods was also highlighted by Katigula (1976), Ezekiel (1978), Jarvis (1979) and Tume ya Rais ya Elimu (1982). There is, seemingly, a vicious cycle: Low Level Competence in English Methods — Less Confidence in Teaching — Lack of Interest and Commitment — No Effort to Advance — Low Level of Competence.

It has been pointed out (Jarvis, 1979) that some of the contributing factors for the decline in the number of competent teachers of English (as also for other subjects) in the primary schools are that (a) many teachers left for Regional and District posts during the move to decentralise; (b) a good number of the competent teachers have qualified after correspondence courses for higher training; (c) after the UPE expansion of schools, there was no corresponding number of qualified teachers to fill the required establishments in all the new schools; and (d) there is a general decline in the prestige of the teaching profession.

English language was even more affected when it was decided that primary school teachers should teach all subjects and that there should be no specialisation. This resulted in teachers with less interest and confidence in the English language having no alternative but to teach it. The effects are even more damaging in the higher classes (V, VI and VII) where some commitment and specialisation in language teaching is needed. Moreover, the frequent changes in syllabi and textbooks in recent years have not only interrupted whatever little progression and consistency there was, but have also put off those teachers who were not conversant enough with the new methods which were being suggested in the new syllabi.

(iii) Low level of education

Another problem associated with the lack of competence is the general low level of education. A teacher ought to have a certain minimum of education. However, during the UPE crash programme, some young people were recruited and trained to be teachers when they themselves had not matured intellectually. Such teachers failed to play their role as educators and leaders adequately. They seemed to lack confidence and a sense of responsibility.

(c) Lack of proper motivation

It is generally agreed that the learning process depends very much on the degree of motivation of the pupils. The writer's interviews with the pupils in the various schools he visited revealed the following:

1. English was generally placed No. 3 as a favourite subject in the lower classes (I–IV) after mathematics and Kiswahili. It was placed No. 3 in the upper classes (V – VII) after mathematics and science.

2. In the lower classes, the reasons for liking or wanting to learn English were mainly: (a) for further academic pursuance, (b) because the teacher was good, (c) in order to speak with relatives and friends.

3. In the upper classes the reasons for liking or wanting to learn English were mainly: (a) further academic pursuance, (b) ability to speak a European language.

4. Most of those who did not list English as one of the three favourite subjects thought that it was a difficult subject or the teacher was not good.

5. There was a remarkable correlation between a good teacher in a class and the liking of a subject.

6. Although in general English was one of the favourite subjects in the investigated primary schools (third out of seven main subjects), the picture was different when results for rural schools were separated from those of urban schools. The results were as shown in Table 7.2.

   Table 7.2 shows that urban primary school pupils placed English as second (after Kiswahili) in their line of preference, whereas the rural primary school pupils on the average placed it fifth (after mathematics, geography, science and Kiswahili). This

TABLE 7.2

Subject	Rural primary schools	Urban primary schools
	%	%
Mathematics	32	24
Kiswahili	13	27
Geography	19	8
Science	18	11
English	12	25
Political education	5	3
History	1	2
Total	100	100

supports the writer's earlier statement on the attitude towards English in the rural primary schools. Moreover, in many of the rural schools the negative attitude towards English was also largely due to unsatisfactory teaching methods and teaching aids.

As a result it may be confidently stated that the main source of interest and motivation for the pupils depended largely on the teacher's handling of the class as well as the availability of appropriate teaching materials. This was more evident, especially, in the lower classes where the pupils had not begun considering the possibilities of further advancement in education or of the need to know more about, or communicate with, the outside world. Such sources of motivation are significantly different from the type of motivation which was in existence during the colonial days when English was highly prestigious in schools because it was the key to white-collar jobs as well as social promotion.

The question of insufficient motivation has also been attributed to lack of clear aims of teaching English so that it became very difficult to motivate the pupils (Ezekiel, 1978). My personal experience in the field is that the majority of teachers teach English because they have to. There is generally no proper attachment to the subject or special aims intended except for the fulfilment of what is in the syllabus. This was also remarked by the Tume ya Rais ya Elimu (1982).

When the pupils were asked whether they had any opportunity to talk or use English at all outside the classroom, they reported that they used English in the situations listed in Table 7.3. However, when examining the table one should realise that the figures do not show the impact of the activity. It is certain that some pupils claimed that they used English to talk

TABLE 7.3

Opportunities of using English	Percentage of the pupils inteviewed
In the lower classes	
1. talking with fellow pupils	32
2. talking to teachers	0
3. talking to parents/relatives	8
4. revising lesson notes in English	11
5. listening to radio	4
6. reading newspapers	0
7. reading books	14
In the upper classes	
1. talking with fellow pupils	66
2. talking to teachers	8
3. talking to parents/relatives	12
4. revising lesson notes in English	78
5. listening to radio	8
6. reading newspapers	8
7. reading books	18

with friends when actually they uttered a few isolated English words while talking Kiswahili or one of the vernacular languages.

(d) Lack of proper language impact

Compared to the English language situation about 15 years ago, the impact of the language at primary school level has very much lessened. This is mainly because of the change of its status in the country. The reduction in the impact of the language has especially been the result of (i) the reduction in the number of periods per week from 12 to only five or six, (ii) its being replaced by Kiswahili in the higher classes as medium of instruction in the classroom and communication outside the classroom, (iii) its being practised very rarely outside the classroom, partly because of the generally ambivalent attitude towards it and partly because practically all primary schools are day schools so that the pupils do not have much time together outside the classroom. Most confessed that they rarely spoke English outside the classroom. This is very different from the situation 25 years ago when pupils in classes VI, VII and VIII were punished when they were found in the school compound speaking languages other than English. According to Tume ya Rais ya Elimu (1982) many young people were afraid to practise their English in public for fear of being considered as still having a colonial hang-over. (iv) It is evident that the number of pupils per class is rather too large for an effective learning situation. According to the research findings, the number of pupils per class ranged from 29 to 48. The average was 39 pupils. This made it difficult for the teacher to involve each pupil in effective language drills or intensive language training.

(e) No clear objectives

Although the lack of clear objectives for teaching and learning English is not the only major problem, the effects of it have a considerable bearing on the four problems mentioned above. The financial and manpower commitment in buying teaching materials in English and in training English language teachers will depend very much on the role and place accorded to the English language. Most English language teachers and language officials are not very clear as to the present status of the English language and its future position in the country. This has the following effects:

1. It is very difficult to plan viable and long-term language methodology.

2. It is difficult to publish school books written in English in any good numbers for fear that by the time they are published English will have ceased to be the language of communication in the secondary schools.

3. The element of ambivalence or contradiction has remained. Should English language teaching be aimed at every pupil in primary school or only those who will eventually need it in their professional life?

4. It is difficult for the government to commit itself materially and in terms of manpower if it is not clear what importance or role English has in the country.

5. It is difficult for the English language experts to advise on the form or type of English which should be taught in the country if the objectives are not clear.

6. One of the reasons for the lack of motivation in the pupils is that many schools and teachers are indifferent about the language because of the lack of a clear statement on the future role of English in the country.

So far there are only two functions of English which could be relevant to all pupils in primary schools. These are:

1. To have access to technical and scientific knowledge and progressive political thought not yet available in Kiswahili;

2. To appreciate the cultures of other peoples, and especially great literature from many other countries which has been translated into English.

It might therefore be useful to emphasise these aims when the policy makers determine the main objectives for teaching and learning English in primary schools.

General Comments and Suggestions

Having established that the most crucial problems facing the teaching and learning of English in primary schools are the lack of: (a) textbooks, reference books and subsidiary or simplified reading materials; (b) competence on the part of the teachers; (c) motivation on the part of the pupils and the absence of commitment on the part of the teachers; (d) proper impact; and (e) clear objectives, we could assume that if solutions could be found to these problems, there is a good chance for significant improvement of the situation. The following are therefore my personal comments and suggestions on each of the problems.

(a) The question of teaching materials

Since the most crucial problem is to make sufficient and appropriate textbooks, reference books and supplementary readers available to the pupils as soon as possible, it is important that all efforts and strategies be implemented in order to realise the desired objectives. Hence, the recent creation of the Book Development Council of Tanzania (BAVITA) is in itself a step in the right direction. The aim should be to have, at most, two pupils share one textbook, and to be able to have mini-libraries in every primary school where pupils, especially in the higher classes, could consult dictionaries and grammar books as well as borrow books to read at home. (Of course, these libraries would also stock books in the other disciplines.) A clear-cut language policy would be necessary in order to clarify the issue about the type of books to publish. It is important to know if English is to be taught as a specialist or as a wider-communication language.

It has been suggested that since the teaching materials in English are so scarce, regions be assisted to produce their own reading materials on duplicated paper. Creative and competent teachers could be involved in writing books or manuals. Others (see Kimesera, 1978) have recommended that there should be writing panels. The present writer would endorse the recommendations if the task were undertaken with all commitment and talent. In fact, the new textbook, *Primary English for Tanzania* (Institute of Education, 1982), has proved more useful than most of the textbooks of English which had been produced since independence (according to a good number of teachers who have started using it). This textbook has rectified a number of shortcomings contained in the earlier works.

(b) The question of teachers' competence

The solution to the lack of competent teachers would be to provide the teacher-trainees with adequate time for training and to ensure that they are fully prepared both academically and pedagogically to be teachers. It is not enough to be conversant with teaching methods. Future teachers must also be competent enough to adapt themselves to the various situations they find at school, including the lack of textbooks and reference books. Teachers ought to be creative and insightful.

English language teachers, especially, ought to have a reasonable command of English in order to teach it properly. It is therefore essential that Grade C teachers should be given in-service training in order to make them improve their language proficiency as well as their pedagogical competence. The suggestion by Tume ya Rais ya Elimu that no third promotion should be given to a teacher unless he or she has done more training is a good way to ensure that teachers do not remain academically dormant in their posts.

It has also been suggested (see Muze, 1978: 28; Tume ya Rais ya Elimu, 1982: 2) that in-service courses be organised at District and Regional levels. Such courses could be planned by the Education Inspectorate Zonal Offices and run by language specialists from the higher education institutions in the country. Also KELT and VSO staff could be involved. Teachers' Colleges specialising in English language (e.g. Marangu) could also assist in preparing materials and guidelines for use by English language teachers.

Moreover, it is thought that English teachers for classes V to VII should be specialists in that subject. This is important in view of the need for committed and effective teachers who are able to detect and correct systematically the weaknesses of the pupils at different stages. In fact, there is need for more commitment and professional interest on the part of the teachers. At present, many teachers teach English only because they were assigned that subject by the school or, in the case of headteachers, because nobody else was willing to teach it.

(c) The question of motivation

It has been suggested that in order to motivate the pupils in English language, the textbooks should describe 'situations which socially and intellectually motivate our children to want to use English in order to learn something, in order to do something, in order to be able to express their thoughts, feelings, knowledge and opinions' (Muze, 1978: 20). As the present writer's investigation indicated, the most important source of motivation to learn English at primary school level is not so much the functional or professional needs of the language, but rather the interest that the teacher could cultivate in the pupils through his pedagogical competence.

The teacher should also be able to make the pupils understand that English will still be important for their general educational advancement even if they did not get the chance to go to secondary school. In fact, according to Tume ya Rais ya Elimu, both Kiswahili and English should be considered as essential subjects to all Tanzanians (see Tume ya Rais ya Elimu, 1982: 100).

(d) The question of language impact

In order to increase the impact of English language in the schools we must first of all clarify the ambivalent position about English and require schools to encourage the use and practice of English in their compounds and outside.

In order to intensify the English language impact, schools should:

1. Introduce more English language periods in the upper classes so as to ensure more language activity in the class. This is especially important because, unlike Kiswahili, the pupils have no practice outside the classroom.

2. Have one or two days in a week on which pupils, especially in the

upper classes (V–VII), are required to speak English in the school compound.

3. Organise activities involving English language for the upper classes.

4. Establish mini-libraries (preferably open to all disciplines) where the English language teacher could place any reference books, subsidiary readers and simplified story books. Some of these books could be on loan to pupils for short periods. In order to encourage pupils to read and understand them (especially in the upper classes), pupils could be asked to make oral or written summaries of what they have read.

5. Organise simple discussions and debates for the upper classes and even encourage inter-school debating activities in English.

6. Arrange for pupils to listen to radio programmes in English or special talks by people with good English language command.

7. Think of ways of minimising interruptions of classes.

(e) The question of language policy

The lack of clear objectives is the primary factor which has contributed to the present situation. Nobody is prepared to invest so much in terms of money and manpower in promoting English language if its future is not certain. As Polomé (Polomé & Hill, 1980) puts it, 'so far the policy of teaching English in primary schools has not been seriously questioned' (p. 294). We need to know (i) when Kiswahili will officially become the medium of instruction at the secondary school level, and (ii) whether English will be required for all Tanzanians or for only those who will need it in their professional life.

We know that when Kiswahili became officially the medium of instruction in primary schools in 1967, the target was that by 1974 it would also have become the medium of instruction at secondary school level. The decision by Tume ya Rais ya Elimu (1982) to recommend that, as from January 1985, all classes in secondary schools should be conducted in Kiswahili was bold, but realistic in view of the fact that we need to have a precise timing so that every effort could be focused on how to ensure that by that specific time the basic preparations would have been carried out. However, this recommendation has been rejected by the government.

Also, it is important that a clear policy is established on the future needs for English language. In order to respond to egalitarian principles, it might be argued that each young Tanzanian has a right to some basic knowledge of English (just as he has a right to basic education) which could help him if he decided to advance himself educationally (formally or privately). On the other hand, economic constraints might not make it realistic to teach English to every young person in an effective way. This calls for a possibility of limiting English language training to a few people who might need it professionally, especially in contacts with people from other countries.

Specific Suggestions

Faced with different options which the policy makers might wish to take, the writer would like to make specific suggestions. The relevance of these suggestions will depend on (i) whether or not the medium of communication in secondary schools will remain English in the next 15 years, (ii) whether there is a need to intensify or spread out the teaching of English in the schools, and (iii) whether English should be taught to every young Tanzanian or only to those who might need it professionally (i.e. those who continue with secondary education).

(a) If the medium of communication remains English in the next 15 years (or more)

If the policy makers decided that English language should remain the medium of instruction in secondary schools for the next 15 years or more, one of the two following options might be adopted by the implementers.

Extensive approach

In this option, English language could start being taught as early as class III and spread over five years to class VII.

1. The advantages are: (a) greater exposure to English; (b) cognitive advantage (that is, the earlier the better); (c) less pressure on the other subjects especially in the later years of primary school.

2. The disadvantages are: (a) more costly in terms of manpower and teaching materials; (b) lack of sufficiently skilled manpower so that grade C and UPE teachers might be required; (c) not sufficiently intensive; (d) pupils are still struggling to master their writing and

reading skills as well as Kiswahili language for those from remote rural areas (this used to be the biggest handicap when English was taught from class I).

3. The suggested number of periods could be 5/6 in the lower classes and 7 periods in the upper classes.

4. From I to IV teachers would teach all subjects; however, from V to VII, a specialist teacher in English is desirable.

5. There should be specific behavioural objectives in terms of structures or functions to be mastered. Emphasis should be on all-round language skills including training in reading and writing.

6. The method to be adapted could be in the area of structuralist/ situational.

7. There should be teacher and pupil books for each class. Also workbooks and supplementary readers would be desirable. The teacher's books should be as explicit and as detailed as possible with a variety of activities.

8. A handbook on ELT methodology published commercially should be used as a basis of the methodology component in Teachers' Colleges' English Courses, in-service training, etc. It could also be used as a reference book by serving teachers. It should emphasise practical issues, techniques, teaching aids, pedagogical strategies, etc.

9. Increase Grade A intake but also select for training Grade C teachers with competence in English for more language training. English language specialists in the upper classes should only be Grade A teachers.

10. Inspectors should make sure that pupils gain proper English language foundation in the lower classes as well as acquire the basic language skills when they reach the upper classes.

11. Such pupils might need a month's intensive refresher course when they go to secondary school. A method like 'Learning Through Language' could be appropriate.

Intensive approach

In this option, English language would start in class V and be taught for three years up to class VII.

1. The advantages are: (a) much cheaper in terms of manpower and teaching materials; (b) allow basics to get good ground through intensive course; (c) could use skilled manpower in concentrated manner — this could easily result in greater teacher and pupil motivation; (d) pupils will have already mastered their writing and reading skills as well as the Kiswahili language.

2. The disadvantages are: (a) it would require high period allocation and so greater pressure on the other subjects; (b) there is a danger that three years would be too short since there is not much practice; (c) pupils would be much older, hence less disposed to language learning.

3. The suggested number of periods could be 7/8 in class V, 8/9 in class VI and 9 in class VII.

4. Teachers should be those who have specialised in the teaching of English so as to ensure intensity and continuity.

5. Emphasis should be on all language skills including training in reading and writing.

6. The method to be adapted should also be structuralist/situational.

7. Each class should have its own teachers' and pupils' books, workbooks and supplementary readers.

8. A handbook on ELT methodology is also important.

9. The teachers should be Grade A holders who qualified well in English and who chose to teach English as their specialist subject.

10. Inspectors should ensure that the teachers are well committed and have good pedagogical skills.

11. Such pupils will also need a refresher course before joining secondary school.

(b) If the medium of communication changes to Kiswahili in the foreseeable future

In case Kiswahili soon becomes the medium of instruction in secondary schools, then the role of English will be reduced to limited educational or functional needs. However, it would be essential to decide between maximalist and minimalist approaches.

Maximalist approach

This approach could be adopted if we wish to give enough basic skills in English to all young people who finish primary school for their future educational or functional needs. It is therefore important to determine the basic English language skills needed by such people. The most obvious ones are reading skills, since one might wish to read books, relevant documents and newspapers in English so as to advance academically. In this case, English could be taught in classes V to VII.

1. The advantages are: (a) everyone would be given a fair chance to advance in one international language; (b) the principle of equality would be maintained since in principle every pupil would have an opportunity to learn some basic English; (c) this would provide good ground for those who will use it as a reading language in secondary school.

2. The disadvantages are: (a) it may prove unnecessarily and unjustifiably costly to teach it in all primary schools, in terms of manpower and teaching materials; (b) many pupils will lack motivation since they will not see its immediate advantages; (c) many teachers will not be committed enough, especially because there would be a need for good pedagogical strategies as well as motivation drives.

3. This would require at least five periods a week.

4. It would be preferable to have a subject specialist in English, but also qualified to teach other subjects.

5. Emphasis should be laid on reading skills as well as functional English.

6. The approach should be functional/communicative.

7. Special books should be prepared. Also there should be many reference books and supplementary reading materials.

8. A handbook of ELT methodology could be useful.

9. The teachers should preferably be Grade A holders with special training in functional or specialist English.

10. Regular evaluation tests should be conducted in schools to ensure that the pupils acquire adequately the basic functional skills.

Minimalist approach

This approach could be adopted if we decided to teach English language only to those who might need it in their professional life. In this case English will start to be taught intensively in secondary schools, especially in the lower classes.

1. The advantages are: (a) it will be much cheaper, in terms of manpower and teaching materials, to teach it only in secondary schools; (b) most pupils will be highly motivated because of the need of English for reading books written in English; (c) most teachers will be specialists and committed people.

2. The disadvantages are: (a) it will deprive those who could not go to secondary school of the chance of pursuing further studies in English medium; (b) the principle of equality will not be respected since English will tend to be an élitist feature; (c) it will retard those in secondary schools in reading books written in English; (d) English may find itself competing with other foreign languages like French and Spanish which are regarded as more peripheral than English for historical reasons.

3. Up to nine periods per week in the first three years of secondary school would be required.

4. The teachers must be specialists in English with special training in functional English.

5. Apart from the purely linguistic skills, a variety of situations corresponding to the various school subjects should be presented.

6. The approach should be functional/communicative with a structuralist/situational base.

7. Appropriate books should be written. Also reference grammar books, dictionaries and supplementary reading materials should be made available in every school.

8. Teachers' reference materials on methodology, language and literature could be useful.

9. The teachers could be diploma or degree holders who have specialised in English language teaching.

Conclusion

As a conclusion one needs to stress the importance of having a clear language policy which will specify the future role of English. Once we know why and how much we need English language, then we can determine how much to invest in terms of manpower and material input. It is this investment which, as is shown in Figure 7.1, will ultimately determine the output in terms of performance in English language by the pupils.

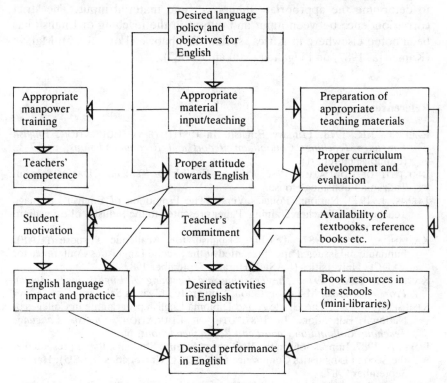

FIGURE 7.1 *Relationship between policy and performance in language (English)*

If the recommendations contained in Tume ya Rais ya Elimu are adopted, then, as the document advocates, both Kiswahili and English should be used by and among Tanzanians to communicate among themselves and with outsiders. They should also gain access, through these languages, to scientific and technical knowledge from other nations.

Whether the nation adopts the recommendations of Tume ya Rais ya Elimu or any other policy on the English language, it is important to take note of the fact that the desired output will always correspond to the input we invest. On the other hand, the amount of investment will depend on the importance we give to the decision — hence the need for clear objectives.

In this respect, one could argue that the standards of English have not necessarily fallen, but rather the general proficiency in English has changed proportionally to the new position the country has implicitly accorded the English language. What one needs to do now is to clarify this position so as to determine the appropriate manpower and material input. The strict correspondence between input and output in the teaching of English has been noted elsewhere in Africa, such as Zimbabwe (Love, 1987), Malawi (Kamanga, 1987) and Uganda (Mukama, 1987).

References

EZEKIEL, J.R. 1978, Primary English. In INSTITUTE OF EDUCATION, *English Language Teaching: Colloquium Report and Recommendations*, pp. 7–12 (unpublished report).
INSTITUTE OF EDUCATION 1982, *Primary English for Tanzania*. Dar es Salaam: Tanzania Publishing House.
JARVIS, J. 1979, National Policies Versus The Promotion of English Language Teaching and Teacher Training. Paper presented to the Ministry of Education, Dar es Salaam.
KAMANGA, T.M. 1987, Teaching English for Academic Purpose (EAP): Fundamental Issues. Paper presented at the Second Linguistics Conference for SADCC Universities (LASU), Harare, September 1987.
KATIGULA, B.A.J. 1976, *The Teaching and Learning of English in Tanzanian Primary Schools*. MA dissertation, University of Dar es Salaam.
KIMESERA, S. 1978, The Grade A and Diploma English programme in Colleges of National Education. In INSTITUTE OF EDUCATION, *English Language Teaching: Colloquium Report and Recommendations*, pp. 25–7.
LOVE, A. 1987, Impressions in the Writings of Science Students. Paper presented at the Second Linguistics Conference for SADCC Universities (LASU), Harare, September 1987.
MUKAMA, R.G. 1987, Linguistics for National Development: The Case of Uganda. Paper presented at the Second Linguistics Conference for SADCC Universities (LASU), Harare, September 1987.
MUZE, M.S. 1978, Professional Cooperation and Strategies. In INSTITUTE OF EDUCATION, *English Language Teaching: Colloquium Report and Recommendations*, pp. 17–22.
POLOMÉ, E. and HILL, C.P. (eds) 1980, *Language in Tanzania*. Oxford: Oxford University Press.
TUME YA RAIS YA ELIMU (Presidential Commission for Education) 1982, *Ripoti Juu ya Mapendekezo ya Elimu Nchini Tanzania*. Dar es Salaam.
WIZARA YA ELIMU 1982, Hotuba ya Waziri wa Elimu Bungeni katika kikao cha Bajeti kwa makadirio ya Fedha kwa mwaka 1982/83. Dar es Salaam.

8 The training of secondary school teachers of English in Tanzania

Z.M. ROY-CAMPBELL

Introduction

Language is a defining characteristic of national identity both within the context of an ethnic group, in a multilingual society, and in terms of a nation, where there is a common national language, e.g. German and Spanish in Europe, Swahili in Tanzania, Arabic in the Middle East. Consequently, language choice can be a political as well as a social issue. The decision to make Swahili the national language of Tanzania, a society with more than 100 ethnic languages, was based on the desire to break away from the linguistic domination of the society by a European language — English — thus allowing for greater national integration, and to develop further one of the country's indigenous languages — Swahili. It is not within the scope of this chapter to discuss why Swahili was chosen as the national language, but it is necessary to acknowledge that Tanzania is one of the few African countries that has been successful in consolidating linguistic unity through the use of a common language. Of the 53 African states only seven — Somalia, Botswana, Lesotho, Swaziland, Rwanda, Burundi and Tanzania — have a common national language.

Nevertheless, the desire for political, social and economic links with other countries dictated the need for a language other than Swahili to facilitate this link. English appeared to be the most logical choice since the infrastructure for English had already been laid in the society, due to the role of English as the official language and medium of education prior to 1967, when Swahili became the national language. Moreover, it was felt that an abrupt change from English to Swahili as the medium of instruction would not have been feasible, given the lack of adequate Swahili lexis to denote scientific and other subject-specific concepts. Also, there was a lack of teaching materials in Swahili. Thus, the most logical alternative was to introduce Swahili as the medium of instruction at the primary school level, in the first instance, with plans to introduce it at secondary and tertiary levels of education to be implemented at a later date.

According to Bhaiji (1976):

In 1969 the Ministry of National Education sent a circular to all headmasters and headmistresses of all Secondary Schools in Tanzania which discussed the possibilities of introducing Kiswahili as a medium of instruction in Secondary Schools in at least some subjects. The Ministry's circular suggested that Political Education could be taught in Kiswahili in 1969/70, Domestic Science in 1970, History, Geography, Biology, Agriculture and Mathematics in 1971.

Coupled with the plans to introduce Swahili as the instructional medium at post-primary school levels was to have been the preparation of teaching materials in Swahili. At present, textbooks have been written in Swahili for the subjects at the primary school level but are yet to be written for secondary school and higher levels.

Although there have been discussions for more than 15 years on changing the medium from English to Swahili at the secondary school level and above, with specific dates having been suggested for this changeover, English remains the medium of instruction at these levels. Therefore, the present linguistic situation in Tanzania is one where there is a national language — Swahili, a dominant language of education — English, and numerous local languages, e.g. Sukuma, Hehe, Nyakusa, primarily used in village communities.

What, then, are the roles of these different languages in Tanzania? If the primary function of language is that of communication, it is necessary to enumerate the various types of communicative acts which are central to that society and the languages which are used for these situations. This becomes even more central in a multilingual society, like Tanzania, since the various languages used serve different communicative functions for multilingual persons in that society. Code-switching (changing from one language to another) is a common feature in the Tanzanian linguistic context, particularly among Swahili speakers. The question here is: what factors determine the language to be used in a given situation? In the case of Tanzania the determining factor was the following directive:

Swahili [should] be used for all Government business, and the use of English or any other foreign languages unnecessarily is to cease forthwith. All Ministries, District Councils, Cooperative Unions, and parastatal organisations are therefore obliged to use Swahili in their day to day business.[1]

Despite this directive, however, English has remained the instructional medium of secondary education. This has created an ambivalent situation where secondary and tertiary level educational institutions are forced to use English in the classroom, while outside the classroom Swahili is used. Moreover, it is not uncommon to see various signs or notices posted around secondary schools written in Swahili. In one particular school which I recently visited I noticed that the names of certain rooms, e.g. biology and chemistry labs, library, were written in Swahili. Thus the problematic of the function of English in Tanzania becomes even more central.

Another side to this question relates to the present economic situation of the country which renders access to educational resources (particularly books from outside the country) exceedingly difficult. This forces schools to rely on insufficient copies of often outdated books as a means of providing their students with access to the instructional medium. The implications of this will be discussed later.

It is within this context that the use of English as a medium of instruction and the training of teachers of English must be viewed. This chapter will briefly examine the functions of English in Tanzania at present, then discuss the training of secondary school teachers of English in an environment where there is an ambivalence towards English. The anomaly of teachers being trained in Literature in English at the University while being expected to teach English language in the schools will also be considered. In addition, the implications of the nature of the training received by these teachers will be discussed.

Use of English in Tanzania

There is no question about the depth of Swahili language in Tanzanian society. Swahili is the most widely used language in Tanzania whether one goes to the Central Post Office, the bank, the law courts or the staff rooms of secondary schools. This is definitely in keeping with the government directive that English should not be used 'unnecessarily'. One question which quite logically arises from this is: what function does English serve in the society? It is the medium of instruction in all secondary schools and most tertiary institutions, thus it is important in those institutions where it is used. Lack of proficiency in this medium can lead to a failure to gain access to the knowledge reproduced in that language. If large sections of learners fail to grasp the knowledge made available to them in the schools due to the language barrier, what then is the purpose of their education?

Falling standards in the use of English at all levels of education are becoming increasingly evident in Tanzania.[2] Although the extent of these falling standards has yet to be empirically quantified and qualified, the plethora of dissertations, colloquia reports, seminar papers and undergraduate projects addressing this issue generally agree that students' knowledge of English, the medium of instruction, is poor and that the teaching of English is unsatisfactory.[3] This lowering of standards of English has a direct relationship to the vast number of students who may gain very little after four years of secondary education. Past examination results for the 'O' Level (Form IV) reveal that in some schools more than 50% of the students fail to gain even a D grade.[4]

A crucial question arising from this issue relates to the source of the problem. Without empirical data it is difficult to identify the specific source of the problem; however, it would appear that the reluctance of the government to define a clear language policy is one of the factors contributing to its perpetuation. The absence of clear guidelines from the government in a situation where the use of English is de-emphasised yet at the same time it remains the medium of instruction leads to ambivalence on the part of both teachers and students. Some sections of the society view English as being important, particularly for access to other countries as well as to the vast amount of knowledge available in English, while others dispute the importance of English in the society. According to the latter group, English is a colonial language which no longer has an important role in Tanzania. They maintain that only a few Tanzanians travel outside Tanzania, so there is no need to 'force' all Tanzanians to learn English, as the majority of them will never use it. This argument is often used to question the need for teaching English at the primary school level.

The teaching of English in Tanzania is grounded within this linguistic environment, where there is an ambivalence towards English, and teachers of English in Tanzania are themselves products of this milieu. Since teachers of English are the primary instruments through which proficiency in English is effected, a myriad questions may arise pertaining to the preparation of teachers for this phenomenal task. It may be useful at this juncture to contextualise the training of secondary school teachers of English in Tanzania.

Teacher Training

General background of the trainees

Secondary school teachers in Tanzania are normally required to possess a Diploma in Education from a College of Education or a BA/BSc Degree with Education from the University. Minimum qualification for admission to both the Diploma and Degree courses is the completion of Form VI (Advanced Level); however, the University has higher criteria for admission in terms of the quantity and quality of passes than do the Colleges. It should also be noted that the University course admits in-service students (teachers who have studied privately and have shown some general academic competence).

At the Advanced Level (Forms V and VI) the English course is a linguistics-based one, aiming at providing students with a descriptive competence of English.[5] It is assumed that the students are adequately proficient in English since they should have passed 'O'level English in order to have been admitted into the 'A' Level course. In addition to descriptive competence, the course seeks to increase the students' linguistic competence by providing them with opportunities to develop the four skills (listening, speaking, reading and writing) further, as well as to help students appreciate language in its literary use. Thus students are expected to perform a range of listening and speaking activities, e.g. listening to and making speeches, dramatisation; reading a range of books — both fiction and non-fiction; and doing a variety of writing, e.g. creative writing and argumentative writing. With this background, it is expected that students are adequately equipped to embark on a Diploma or Degree course in teacher training. The content of the Diploma and Degree courses differs significantly, so each course will be examined in turn.

The Diploma course

The Diploma course is a two-year programme, offered by Colleges of Education, with an allocation of 200 contact hours per year. There are three variations of this course, each providing students with different depths of the language in different aspects. All three variations basically use the same syllabus, which has five objectives, one academic objective and four professional ones. They include:

1. to develop students' competence and proficiency in English language;

2. to provide the students with an elementary grounding in contemporary approaches in English language teaching;
3. to acquaint them with the English syllabuses in use in the schools and colleges;
4. to train them in methods of teaching the topics in the syllabuses;
5. to ensure that they are capable of producing aids and materials for teaching.[6]

This course seeks to integrate the academic (objective 1) and methodological aspects (objectives 2–5) of the course. It is divided into four major components — the Applied Linguistics Component, the Structure Component, the Phonology Component, and the Reading and Writing Component — and includes a section on Professional Skills (evaluation, schemes of work, language teaching aids, department organisation).

It should be noted here that the English course is one among several optional courses from which the trainees must choose. Secondary school teachers in Tanzania are normally required by the Ministry of Education to have two teaching subjects, so English is combined with another teaching subject. Consequently, the students' course load includes Psychology of Education (Malezi) which is taught in Swahili, English (option) and another subject (e.g. History, Swahili, Political Education (Siasa) etc.). Students must therefore divide their study time between English and three other subjects. Most of the other subjects are taught through the medium of English, except for Swahili, Malezi and Siasa. However, if a student happens to be studying English in addition to Swahili or Siasa, then the amount of exposure to English will necessarily be limited.

According to the syllabus, the English course is *'an integrated one dealing with the main structures of the English language and the methods for teaching them'*[7] (my emphasis). Fifteen topics are listed, e.g. Noun Phrase, Verb Phrase, Clauses (Concession, Result, Purpose, etc.), Direct and Reported Speech. Trainees' own proficiency in English is expected to improve by demonstration lessons, practice in designing lesson plans and materials to go with them, and micro-teaching practice dealing with the topics they will be expected to teach. In addition, the syllabus stipulates that 'additional help will be planned for those students who have difficulty in using certain structures'.[8] The other two components, the phonology and the reading and writing components, also provide opportunities for the trainees to improve their proficiency in English. The effects of this course upon the trainees will be discussed later; let us now turn to the structure of the degree course.

The Degree course

At the University trainee teachers of English are enrolled in the Education Stream of the Faculty of Arts and Social Sciences, and are required to take two teaching subjects. These may include Literature in English, History, French, Swahili, Political Science, etc., in addition to English. Moreover, students have the option to take English as a major or minor subject. The number of content courses for minors is about half that of the majors. Courses in English are done in the Department of Foreign Languages and Linguistics. Students are also required to take courses in the Department of Education as well as the Department of their other teaching subject. Let us now take a brief look at the courses which these students are required to take in the Department of Foreign Languages and Linguistics.

All majors in English do General Linguistics courses in all three years of their study and a course in Applied Linguistics in their final year. Minors, however, are required to take only the first year General Linguistics course and Applied Linguistics in their third year.

In their first year all students of English do a course in Structure, Usage and Spoken English. This course provides a description of English grammar and structure, theory and practice in segmental phonemes of English and an introduction to English intonation and pronunciation. In addition, first-year students take a course in Communication Skills, which is aimed at improving students' proficiency in coping with the requirements of academic study in English.

During their second year they study English Structure, a course involving an analysis of structure, discussions of the meaning of the structures and practice in their use. In addition, English majors take a course in English Usage, which is an introduction to language variety, levels of language and various registers of English. Students in this course are provided with extensive writing practice. Minors in English are required to study this course in their third year. Third-year students majoring in English are required to do a course in Structure, Function and Style, including work in syntactic structure, lexical choice and semantics.

Coupled with the English courses, all students are required to do a methodology course, which is in effect equivalent to half a course (i.e. 30 hours instead of 60 hours allocated to full courses). This course, offered by the Department of Education, seeks to help the students develop various types of classroom techniques and activities for the teaching of English, and to assist students in the development of teaching materials for use in the schools. The different components of the secondary school syllabus are examined and students are exposed to and receive limited practice in various techniques for teaching these components, i.e. Oral-Aural Skills, Structures, the Reading Programme and the Writing Programme.

At this point, it is important to note another group of students who are expected to be teachers of English once they complete their University studies. These are students who combine Literature in English with another teaching subject, other than English. The assumption here is that a teacher who has been trained in Literature in English should also be able to teach English Language. It is interesting to note that the Literature programme does not include any courses in English language; rather it focuses on different aspects and themes of literature written in English. Part of the training of these students includes a course in methodology, but its focus is more on the teaching of literature rather than language. The implications of this anomalous situation will be considered later.

Having described the training programmes for teachers of English, I shall now attempt to evaluate the adequacy of this training within the sociolinguistic environment outlined earlier.

How adequate is this training?

From the description of the preparation of secondary school teachers of English, it would appear that the only stage in which they are taught English Language is at the secondary school level, particularly Forms I to IV (and to a limited extent in primary school). Although the 'A' level course provides students with advanced practice in the four skills, it concentrates on helping students to recognise patterns, then to describe them using appropriate terminology. This is in contrast to the 'O' level course which should provide students with an ability to use English in situations in which they need to use the language. One problem, however, is that in many cases the 'O' level syllabus is taught as the 'A' level syllabus should be, i.e. students are taught about the language. Thus when asked to recognise or produce a specific aspect of grammar they may quite easily do this; but when asked to express themselves on a given topic, using the language which they have learned, many students fail to do this satisfactorily. When one also takes into account the sociolinguistic environment, one in which very little English is heard outside the classroom, it is not surprising that these students are not adequately proficient in English. Proficiency can only be achieved with practice, both within and outside the classroom.

Being cognisant of the situation described above, one could then argue that many entrants to the Diploma course lack adequate proficiency in English. This point is corroborated by Moshi (1984) who contends that

'One of the main problems with courses for English language teachers is that they are not sufficiently emphatic of the need for the teacher trainee to be conversant with the language'. It is against this background that the adequacy of the training courses for teachers of English must be viewed. At this juncture it would be useful to note the views of teachers who have undergone this training about the adequacy of the Diploma course in preparing them for their roles in the schools.

Ex-diploma students' perceptions of the course

In the effort to elicit the views of former students of the Diploma course, questionnaires were distributed to students currently studying English with Education at the University of Dar es Salaam. Of the 70 questionnaires which were distributed, 45 were returned, and only 22 of these students had had training in English teaching prior to joining the University. Table 8.1 indicates the type of pre-University training of these students. As can be observed from Table 8.1, the majority of the respondents had done the Diploma in Education course, described earlier, while six had done both the Diploma and the Certificate courses. It would appear that the latter group have upgraded themselves from Grade A primary school teachers to secondary school teachers of English. Only two of the respondents had not had any previous training.

TABLE 8.1 Pre-university qualifications of trainee teachers of English

Certificate of Education	2
Diploma in Education	11
Both Certificate and Diploma	6
Certificate of Education and Diploma in TEFL[a]	1
None	2

[a] This is a short course done overseas (Teaching English as a Foreign Language)

The teaching experience of these former teachers ranges from 1 to 12 years, with the majority of them (13) having taught for at least two years prior to joining the University. Table 8.2 indicates the level/s at which they have taught. The majority of these students, as can be seen, had had experience teaching at the secondary school level, while three had had experience as teacher trainers before joining the Degree course.

TABLE 8.2 Teaching levels

Primary only	3
Secondary only	14
Primary and secondary	2
Primary and teacher training college	2
All 3 levels	1

In addition to seeking information about their background, the questionnaires asked the respondents to indicate whether or not they felt their training was adequate for the job they were expected to do. Of the 22 students, 16 felt that their training was inadequate. They felt that they lacked the following aspects:

1. good teaching methods
2. guidelines on the organisation of the content
3. understanding of some of the topics in the syllabus
4. communication skills
5. basic knowledge of grammar
6. mastery of the language
7. fluency in the language
8. correct pronunciation in the language.

These aspects can be divided into two groups: pedagogic factors and linguistic ones. Most of the respondents expressed concern at their own levels of proficiency in English, attributing this to a poor background in English. This point would tend to substantiate the contention that many trainees lack adequate proficiency in English when they join the Diploma course, while at the same time implying that the Diploma course does not *provide* them with adequate proficiency in the language.

Related to the inadequate preparation of teachers are the problems which they encounter in teaching English. Problems listed by the respondents include:

1. lack of textbooks, reference books, resource materials
2. inadequate time allocated for English in the school timetable
3. lack of learning attitude and interest on the part of the students
4. curriculum is above the students' level
5. poor background of the students (far below the required standard)
6. teaching English in English.

These problems can be divided into administrative, political and pedagogic, although there is a clear inter-relationship between them. The third problem can be seen as a bridge between the administrative and pedagogic problems, since attitudes and interest are related to perceptions of what is important. Lack of instrumental motivation for the learning of English, despite the fact that it is the medium of instruction, arises from the sociolinguistic environment which has ostensibly de-emphasised the importance of English in the society. With the rise of Swahili as the national language and its institutionalisation as the official language and medium of primary education, coupled with the anticipation that Swahili would eventually replace English at all other levels of education, English has ceased to be a necessary language for the majority of Tanzanians. This is why one rarely hears English spoken by Tanzanians outside the classroom, except when they are communicating with certain non-Tanzanians.

Related to this is the first problem, particularly the lack of books. Exposure to language can be through the visual medium — the written word — or through the oral medium — the spoken word. Despite lack of extensive exposure in one of these media, learners can manage to achieve an adequate proficiency in the language, either a speaking ability or a reading ability. However, when extensive exposure in both media is absent, one can hardly expect a learner to develop adequate proficiency in the language. Although the shortage of books is partially a problem of inadequate foreign exchange, it can also be attributed to the failure of competent Tanzanians to write books in English to be used in the schools. Not only do students need textbooks for their various subjects, they also need access to many types of books, at appropriate levels. This will ensure that despite their limited exposure to the oral language, they will be able to become proficient in receiving written information.

Problems 5 and 6 reinforce each other and are intricately linked with the other problems. Inadequate exposure to English at the primary school level has led to the situation where many Form I students (first year of secondary school) neither understand spoken English nor are able to write a grammatical English sentence. The syllabus which the secondary school teachers are expected to teach assumes that their students have a basic foundation in English, at least a familiarity with certain words and structures.

Owing to this inability of their students to understand simple English, some teachers have found it difficult to teach English in English. Although this has been listed as a problem, I would contend that it is not a problem. In fact, within the present context obtaining in Tanzania where English is not a part of the normal linguistic environment, I would argue that it is necessary to use Swahili when teaching English, particularly where it can help to clarify points not clearly understood in English. This, of course, has serious implications for the role of English in the society (see Chapter 6, this volume).

Having assessed the Diploma course from the point of view of the learners, let us now examine more closely the training received by teachers of English at the University of Dar es Salaam.

University-trained teachers of English

We have already seen the structure of the Degree course and noted the varying depths of exposure to English of the students, depending on whether they major or minor in English. From the description of all the English courses it appears that invariably they focus on descriptive and analytical competence. Similar to the assumptions underlying the 'A' level course, the Degree course assumes that the entrants have an adequate proficiency in English. Although it was noted earlier that the cream of the Form VI leavers are normally the ones accepted into the University, many former teachers, Diploma and Grade A Certificate holders are also admitted into the Degree programme. Are we to assume that all of these students have an adequate level of proficiency in English? Experience of teaching these students has shown that many of them do not possess such proficiency. Bearing in mind the comments made earlier about the 'O' level and 'A' level courses, this should not be surprising, as these students are but products of the same system.

The Diploma course appears to recognise that many students may lack adequate proficiency in English, so it seeks to help them improve their own language by providing activities around the topics which the trainees will be required to teach. This is not the case with the University course. Some of the structures the students will be required to teach (according to the syllabus) are dealt with in their English courses, but from a theoretical point of view rather than a practical one. The methodology course, which is the place where the techniques for teaching the structures as well as the other aspects of the syllabus are taught, has an insufficient time allocation to allow for many of the grammatical structures to be dealt with adequately. Thus, we could say that the University course does not seek to improve the students' proficiency in English; rather it aims at providing students with knowledge about the language.

It is my contention that knowledge about the language, without adequate proficiency in using it, leads a teacher in turn to teach his or her students about the language rather than providing them with much practice in using the language. When visiting secondary school English classrooms it is not uncommon to find this situation. This, of course, serves only to perpetuate the situation described earlier, where students learn about the language and have very little opportunity for using it. If we then consider the case of the literature teachers who are forced to teach English, the problem becomes even more compounded. One would normally expect that a student of literature in English should be quite proficient in the language, otherwise how could he or she analyse various literary texts? This is indeed an intriguing question. During my four years as Literature Methods tutor at the University of Dar es Salaam, I have encountered a number of students of Literature who were not adequately proficient in spoken or written English. Despite this, upon completion of their studies at the University they were posted to schools as teachers of English. The reason for this apparent anomaly is evident; there is an inadequate number of teachers of English in the schools and Literature in English is no longer a part of the secondary school curriculum, except in a few schools (less than 10). Instead of being offered as a subject in its own right, a literary component has been incorporated into the English language courses as the Reading Programme.

This problem of literature teachers being required to teach English in the schools is related to a wider problem. As noted above there is a shortage of English teachers in the schools. In many schools the English teachers are very overloaded, sometimes having as many as 25 periods per week. Such a teacher may have five different groups of 40 students each. Can one really expect such a teacher to provide his or her students with adequate practice in using the language? This becomes even more daunting when one considers the other responsibilities of the teacher, both within and outside the school. One question which might be posed here is: *why* is there a shortage of teachers of English? This question may partially be answered by noting the number of teachers of English who have been trained by the University of Dar es Salaam over the past 19 years (see Table 8.3).

From Table 8.3 we can observe that over the past 19 years 374 *qualified* teachers of English have been trained at the University. By qualified I mean those who have studied English as a subject. Of these, 329 were Tanzanians. The exact or approximate number of these teachers who are still in the secondary schools (or who ever reached them) is not known at present. However, it is worth noting that many of the present Tanzanian members of staff of the Departments of Foreign Languages and Linguistics, Literature and Theatre Arts, as well as a few members of other Departments, e.g. Education and the Institute of Education (English Panel), are included in this figure.

When we add to this the number of Literature-trained teachers of

TABLE 8.3 *Total numbers of students registered for English and/or Literature at the University of Dar es Salaam from 1967 to 1986*

Year of Graduation	English	Graduates in: Literature	Both	Total
1967	8	4	3	15
1968	3	8	1	12
1969	15	13	4	32
1970	19	16	3	38
1971	27	5	7	39
1972	41	5	10	56
1973	42	5	3	50
1974	24	15	6	45
1975	11	27	4	42
1976	11	24	4	39
1977	12	25	6	43
1978	10	17	10	37
1980	5	19	11	35
1981	6	22	6	34
1982	3	15	6	24
1983	10	21	5	36
1984	5	14	3	22
1985	5	10	5	20
1986	12	10	8	30
TOTALS	269	275	105	649

Source: Taken from a survey carried out by the Interdepartmental Committee on the Improvement of the Teaching of English, based at the University of Dar es Salaam. Compiled by Y.Y. Mcha, Department of Foreign Languages and Linguistics, University of Dar es Salaam.

English we have 649, nearly double the number of English-trained teachers. It is not difficult to see, therefore, why the Ministry of Education requires Literature teachers to teach English in the schools, particularly when one considers that the policy makers there may not be aware of the content of the Literature programme, i.e. that it does not include any courses in language.

To gain an estimation of the proportion of students who opt to study English, as opposed to other subjects at the University, let us look more closely at the enrolment of students from 1983 to 1985. The total number of education students in the Faculty of Arts and Social Science, who enrolled in 1983 and completed their course in 1986, is 98. Of these, 74 were in the secondary education stream and 29% of them (22) had studied English. For the 1984 group, out of a total of 112 students, 80 were in the secondary education stream with 25% (20) studying English. During the academic year 1985, 157 students registered as education students and 30% of them (47) studied English. (The exact numbers of those who would either major or minor in English in the secondary stream were not available for this group at the time of writing.)

From the above figures and Table 8.3 it would appear that the numbers of students opting to train as teachers of English has been increasing since 1985, as compared to the small numbers of students who trained as English teachers between 1980 and 1984. However, the quality of teachers is as important as their quantity. This section has suggested that the training is inadequate, given the sociolinguistic environment in which these teachers are trained. Arising from this is the question: what is adequate training for a teacher of English? The next section will briefly address this question.

Who is an adequately trained teacher of English?

It is generally accepted that language teacher competence can be divided into two types: pedagogic competence and linguistic competence. Knowledge about the language may fall somewhere between these two types of competence, since a person may on the one hand be proficient in English, as a result of extensive practice in using the language, but lack knowledge of how the language is organised, while on the other hand he may be knowledgeable about how the language is organised, yet be unable to express himself adequately in English.

Many teachers of English being trained in Tanzania at present would appear to fall into the latter category. As has earlier been discussed, their training provides them with a wealth of knowledge about English but with very little opportunity for using it in meaningful ways. Thus, we might contend that many teachers lack adequate proficiency in English.

This, however, begs the question: what is adequate proficiency in English? Proficiency, or communicative competence, cannot be divorced from context, the Tanzania context being a foreign/second language one. In discussing language competence, Strevens (1972) has designated a 4-level scale of competence for second/foreign language situations: threshold of intelligibility, locally acceptable, internationally acceptable, and native-like ability, specifying 'internationally acceptable' as a reasonable target for teachers of English. Kachru (1981), on the other hand, maintains that

communicative competence is partially determined by 'culture-bound para-
meters, and the concepts of *acceptability, appropriateness*, and intelligibility
cannot be used independently in this context' (his emphasis). As I have
pointed out in another discussion (Roy-Campbell, 1985) Tanzanian curriculum developers, educators and policy makers must decide what level they
want to achieve in the Tanzanian context. This decision, however, must be
guided by careful consideration of the role of English in Tanzania.

Once what should be taught to the learners has been determined, it will
be easier to determine the minimal acceptable level of proficiency for the
teacher. For example, if it is agreed that students need to be proficient in all
four skills, then the teacher must be fluent in English with an acceptable
pronunciation of the language. While, conversely, if students primarily
require a reading knowledge of the language, then complete fluency of
expression may not be essential for the teacher of English.

Taking into consideration the situation in Tanzania at present, teachers
of English need to be able to express themselves fluently and correctly.
They must be in a position to help their learners develop good language
habits and to serve as a model for learners who may have no other model.
Failure to achieve this minimal level of proficiency would render a teacher
inadequately proficient in English. Coupled with the minimal proficiency
(communicative competence) must be a knowledge about how the language
is organised, in order that the teacher will be able to help the learners see
the interrelationship between the different aspects of the language
(linguistic/pedagogic competence).

Viewing these levels of competence in the light of the training courses
offered for secondary school teachers of English, we find that they provide
trainees with knowledge about the language and exposure to some techniques for teaching the language, but very little training in how to use the
language. Observations of trainees during their block teaching practice
sessions have revealed that much more training, or opportunity for practice
of techniques by the trainees, is also needed for equipping teachers of English
with concrete techniques for developing communicative competence in their
learners, as opposed to teaching their learners about the language.

How, then, can these changes be effected in the teacher training
programme? It is important to note that the suggested changes need to be
achieved at two levels: the first level is to produce more competent teachers
in future Diploma and Degree programmes, while the second level involves
improvement of the competence of teachers already in the field. Level one
is quite straightforward, as it involves altering the teacher training syllabi to
incorporate the suggested changes. However, the second level is more
complex. It involves dealing with experienced teachers already in the

schools. This level could be implemented through in-service courses, where teachers are called in to a given centre for a 2–4 weeks seminar or workshop. Although an obvious issue here is source of funds for the in-service courses, this issue should not deter the effort to improve the competence of our teachers of English.

An additional area to consider in the effort to improve the competence of teachers of English concerns the issue of Literature-trained teachers of English. If one accepts that in the absence of a Literature course in the secondary schools these teachers will be obliged to teach English, then their training programme should be reorganised to take this into account. Recommendations have already been made by the Inter-departmental Committee for the Improvement of the Teaching of English, based at the University of Dar es Salaam, to develop an integrated Language–Literature Programme which would draw courses from the Departments of Foreign Languages and Linguistics, Literature and Education. Although this joint programme has not yet been fully accepted, owing to administrative problems, it is hoped that within the near future it will be incorporated into the training course for teachers of English.

Conclusion

Training teachers of English in an environment where English is infrequently used outside the classroom is a phenomenal task, particularly when learners are expected to use English as a medium of instruction for their other subjects. Neither teacher-trainees nor their students receive sufficient practice in the language to develop adequate competence in using English. The results of this are becoming increasingly evident. Quite recently I was conducting research in various regions of Tanzania into the 'Reading Competence in English of Secondary School Students in Tanzania'.[9] Complaints from teachers that their students 'do not know English' were the order of the day. In fact, this was the major complaint in many of the schools visited. Teachers of subjects other than English were emphatic about the need for their students to be taught how to express themselves correctly in English. Many admitted that some of their students (Forms I–IV) are unable to read and understand the textbooks they use because they do not know English. They acknowledged that there were very few copies of textbooks for their students, in most subjects, thus they are unable to provide the students with sufficient practice in reading in English.

It is, of course, seen as the responsibility of the English teachers to teach their students correct English. Thus, overburdened teachers of English, with very few books at their disposal and very little time to carry out their responsibility (3 hours 20 minutes to 4 hours per week — i.e. five to six 40-minute periods), are even more disadvantaged by their own inadequate competence in the language and appropriate techniques for developing in the students an ability to use the language. Some of the teachers of English whom I interviewed complained that they had been in the schools for ten years or more without any additional input, in the form of short courses, seminars or workshops. Bringing together teachers of English from various schools could yield far-reaching benefits for both the teachers and the schools, as they could jointly develop resources to be used in the schools.

In conclusion, it should be noted that in order for adequate proficiency in English to be developed, learners must be exposed to that language as widely as possible, through visual and/or oral stimuli. In an environment where English is not used, yet remains the medium of instruction, it is expected that learners and teachers alike will encounter enormous difficulties in using the language with adequate proficiency. Improving the teaching of English in this context is indeed a challenge to linguists and educators alike.

Notes to Chapter 8

1. Quoted by H. Olsen, in 'Swahili as an educational medium', *Kiswahili Journal*, Vol. 42, 1972, p. 6.

2. A recent report prepared for the Tanzania Ministry of Education and the British Overseas Development Administration has shown that the levels of proficiency in English at all levels of Education in Tanzania is far below the internationally accepted standard. However, this has not been correlated with earlier levels of proficiency in English in Tanzania. See C. Criper and W. Dodd (1984), *Report On The Teaching of English Language And Its Use As A Medium In Education In Tanzania.*

3. Some of these include B.A.Katigula, *The Teaching and Learning of English in Tanzanian Primary Schools*; MA Dissertation, University of Dar es Salaam, 1975; M.V. Mvungi, *Language Policy in Tanzanian Primary Schools with Emphasis on Implementation*, MA Dissertation, University of Dar es Salaam, 1975, and *The Relationship between Performance in the Instructional Medium and some Secondary School Subjects in Tanzania*, PhD Dissertation, University of Dar es Salaam, 1982; F. Mlekwa, *The Teaching of English In Tanzanian Secondary Schools*, MA Dissertation, University of Dar es Salaam, 1977, *inter alia.*

4. See National Examination Council of Tanzania, *Summary of 'O' Level Results,* for at least the past three years.

5. *English Language Syllabus* for Forms V and VI, Institute of Education, Dar es Salaam, 1982.

6. *Diploma In Education English Option Syllabus* for Dar es Salaam and Morogoro Colleges of National Education, Institute of Education, 1979.

7. *Ibid.*

8. *Ibid.*

9. This research was part of an IDRC-funded project which investigated the 'Reading Competence of Tanzanian Secondary School Students in English', and was carried out in the Department of Foreign Languages and Linguistics of the University of Dar es Salaam by M.P. Qorro and Z.M. Roy-Campbell, 1986/87.

References

BHAIJI, A.F. 1976, The medium of instruction in our schools. *Papers In Education and Development,* No. 3, University of Dar es Salaam.

CRIPER, C. and DODD, W. 1984, *Report On The Teaching of English Language And Its Use As A Medium In Education In Tanzania.* Dar es Salaam: The British Council.

INSTITUTE OF EDUCATION 1972, *Diploma In Education English Option Syllabus.* Dar es Salaam: Institute of Education.

— 1979, *English Language Syllabus For Forms 5 and 6.* Dar es Salaam: Institute of Education.

KACHRU, B.B. 1981, The pragmatics of non-native varieties of English. In L.E. SMITH (ed.) *English For Cross Cultural Communication.* Hong Kong: Macmillan Press Ltd.

MOSHI, E.A. 1984, Problems of Teaching English In Colleges of National Education. (Mimeo.) Dar es Salaam: Institute of Education.

ROY-CAMPBELL, Z.M. 1985, Teaching English as a medium of instruction: An integrative approach. *Studies In Curriculum Development,* No. 3.

STREVENS, P. 1972, Improving the teacher's own English. In G.E. PERREN (ed.) *Teachers of English As A Second Language; Their Training and Preparation.* London: Cambridge University Press.

9 Can a foreign language be a national medium?

H.R. TRAPPES-LOMAX

Introduction

> The forces of conservation and change [may] have to be reconciled, and
> stability achieved, by deliberate policy decisions. It might, for example,
> be decided to have the mother tongue used as a medium of instruction in
> the primary school so as to ensure that the child's educational develop-
> ment is rooted in his own cultural heritage, and then transfer to a foreign
> language as the medium for secondary education.
> (Criper & Widdowson, 1975)

The situation described in this passage is approximately that which has
prevailed in Tanzania for the past 20 years, except (i) that the terms
'authenticity' and 'modernity' (e.g. Whiteley, 1971: 156) might be more apt
than 'conservation' and 'change', since in Tanzania the 'authentic' language
— Swahili — is, or has been, the one associated with change, while use of
the language of modernity — English — may be, or has been, more readily
associated with a certain sort of conservatism; (ii) Swahili, though the
language of all, is mother tongue, in a strict sense, for relatively few; (iii) the
distribution of educational functions between Swahili (primary and teacher
training) and English (secondary and tertiary) is not, and never was
intended to be, 'stable'; and (iv) the use of the term 'foreign' in this context
begs a rather crucial language planning question which it is my purpose in
this chapter to examine. In undertaking this examination, I shall address
first the general issues, then the particular case of Tanzania.

Language Status and Language Medium

What should a national medium of education do?

It is noted by Bull (1964) that 'while getting educated is a personal matter, in contrast, providing education is a social enterprise'. A medium of education, therefore, as an essential part of the larger process, must (a) enable learners to get educated and (b) enable society to educate. In the former capacity it should, ideally, adequately fulfil each of the four functions of language for the individual described by Le Page (1964). These are (i) communion, (ii) expression, (iii) conceptualisation and (iv) communication. Getting educated is not just a matter of receiving and imparting information (iv), but also of learning to think and thinking (iii), reacting demonstratively to experience (ii) and relating to teachers and fellow learners (i). As a medium of educating, it should (i) make attainable the educational objectives — political, cultural, economic, ideological, religious — of society; (ii) do so universally, and equally for all; and (iii) do so efficiently and economically.

If so, what should a national medium of education be?

We may usefully distinguish (in line with Stern, 1983: 9) between those characteristics of a language which are relatively objective (or constant) and those which are subjective (or variable). The objective characteristics required of a medium of education fall under the general heading of standardisation. The language should be 'codified' (to minimise non-functional variation), 'elaborated' (to enable it to cope with as wide a range of functions as required) and 'written' (so that people should have something to read in it). In general, the higher up the educational system a language is to be used, the more 'standardised' it needs to be.

The subjective characteristics required of a medium of instruction are: (i) that it should be *accepted* by all concerned (parents, teachers, pupils and society at large) as suitable for its assigned role and of such functional importance as to be worth the effort of acquiring: this is the attitudinal factor and, as frequently observed, it has an important bearing on motivation; (ii) that it should be *teachable* to the required standard: this is dependent partly on (i), partly on the availability of competent teachers, proficient in the language and equipped with suitable methods and materials, and partly on: (iii) that the language should be *experienced* in use. This 'experience' should, if possible, be prior to as well as concurrent with the use as medium, and the 'use' should involve functions additional to the function as medium. The most energetic arguments for the necessity of such experience have been made in connection with the case for the use of the mother tongue — the language most intimately experienced — in the early years of schooling, but the experience of a 'natural language environment' is a demonstrable prerequisite for 'optimal language acquisition' (Burt & Dulay, 1981) and as such is plainly what is called for whenever progress in the other spheres of education is immediately dependent on satisfactory acquisition of the language as medium. Burt and Dulay define a natural language environment as one which exists 'whenever the focus of the speaker is on the content of the communication rather than on language itself' as, for example, in seeking directions or listening to the news (cf. Gorman's 'situations of interaction and reception', 1971). This is the kind of setting, or 'condition', which in Krashen's terms favours 'acquisition' — informal, free, undirected, naturalistic — over classroom 'learning' (Stern, 1983: 392).

When is a language 'foreign'?

Any language which is non-indigenous to a particular speech community may be called foreign. However, 'the term is usually applied only to languages spoken outside the boundaries in which one lives, or, more crucially, to languages learnt only for communication with those living outside one's own community and not used for everyday communication within one's speech community' (Brumfit & Roberts, 1983). A language which *is* used within the speech community, but which is not the mother tongue of its speakers, is a 'second' language. The three most important possible functions of such a language are (i) as a language of wider communication between speakers of different vernaculars, (ii) as an official language used in public administration, the law and political activity, and (iii) as a language of education (i.e. a medium). A language not fulfilling the first or second of these functions but intended, within the scope of some national language plan, to fulfil the third, would be in a plainly anomalous position: its use as medium underpinned by no second-language function other than itself, and its status therefore, effectively, from the point of view of the educational system, that of a foreign, not a second, language. It is this situation that I have in mind in asking the next question.

Are there any *a priori* reasons for doubting the efficacy of a foreign language as a national medium?

Since it is improbable that a nation would select as its national medium a non-standard foreign language, we may direct our attention to the subjective characteristics required. From what is said above we would be led to hypothesise that a foreign language could be rendered inefficacious as medium by (i) its not being accepted (because it is 'foreign' — it lacks authenticity — and because, outside the educational system, it is functionally unimportant); by (ii) its not being teachable (because, by the nature of the situation, no strong internal support exists for the sustaining of a corps of teachers linguistically proficient as well as professionally equipped to create the conditions requisite for 'learning'); and by (iii) its not being experienced (because its only use is within the educational system — or some part of the educational system — as medium and this may not, in itself, be enough for naturalistic 'acquisition', as a vital or at least highly desirable concomitant of classroom 'learning', to take place).

What are the predictable consequences of the failure of a language as medium?

Referring to our earlier discussion we may summarily list these as follows:

a. for the individual learner:
   — his relations with his teachers and fellow learners, in so far as these require to be mediated by the foreign language medium, will be impoverished;
   — he will have no adequate linguistic means of educated self-expression;
   — he will be handicapped in thinking and in learning to think;
   — he will be able neither to receive nor to impart educative information.

b. for society:
   — the objectives of education will not be achieved;
   — those who, through home environment etc, may have privileged access to the foreign language will be at an unfair advantage in relation to the majority;
   — the cost of failure will be felt in every domain, economic, social and political, as well as in the waste of time and money.

Can the predicted deficiencies of a foreign language medium be planned for and overcome?

Since the predicted deficiencies arise from the subjective characteristics of foreign languages, not those of second languages, a plausible strategy for remedying the problems associated with a foreign language medium could be as follows: create for the foreign language a second-language-like environment so that, in short, it becomes more accepted, more teachable, more experienced in use. This solution, however, may be (a) very costly (in time, money, social effects) and (b) not practicable (because of the persistence of attitudes and habits, and because of underlying weaknesses in the educational system as a whole).

English Medium in Tanzania

The status of English

A visitor to Tanzania in 1988 will *see* English (in the daily newspaper, along shopping streets, on some notices and signs) and could *use* it (in some shops, hotels and public offices) but would not often *hear* it spoken between Tanzanians (except in the presence of foreigners) even if he visited the University (unless he happened to overhear a lecture or a seminar or a departmental, faculty or senate meeting). In this respect (leave aside the departmental meetings etc.) the visitor's experience in Tanzania would be more similar to what he might encounter in Belgium or Sweden than to his likely experience in Kenya or Uganda.

The broad sociolinguistic picture in Tanzania still, it is true, fits approximately into the three-language structure (Nida & Wonderly, 1971) of 'in-group language' (the vernaculars), 'out-group language' (Swahili) and 'language of specialised information' (English), described by Whiteley as 'linguistic trifocalism'; but as Whiteley points out (e.g. 1971: 151) there has been some reallocation of settings, largely at the expense of English (but also at the expense of the vernaculars) and in favour of Swahili, to the extent that it has been frequently observed that, for example, 'English for us is becoming daily more of a foreign language, spoken by very few people' (newspaper article of 1967, quoted in Mlama & Matteru, 1978); or, a less extreme view and probably closer to the true situation, 'English is assuming a position somewhere halfway between a second and a foreign language' (Mbunda *et al.*, 1980: 294). A Handbook for English Teachers, issued by the Institute of Education in 1969, observed: 'For the time being English is still used as a medium of communication in Tanzania, although on an ever decreasing scale, for a limited number of purposes.' In 1988, except where contacts with non-Swahili speakers are involved, and except in one remaining major second-language function, these purposes are virtually extinct. The remaining function is: to be the medium of secondary and higher education.

I shall not here explore the origins of this shift, except to note that for the historian of sociolinguistic change, the events of 1967 — the year of the Arusha Declaration and of Education for Self-Reliance — provide a fascinating focus of interest. The National Swahili Council was established, for the purpose of promoting Swahili in all spheres of national life. The Second Vice-President declared that 'Swahili should be used for all government business and the use of English or any other foreign language unnecessarily is to cease forthwith' (Mohamed, 1975). And Swahili was made the medium of instruction throughout primary education (it had previously been used in the first four years) with the clear expectation and intention that it would eventually replace English throughout the educational system. Voicing the spirit which motivated these decisions, the Dean of the Faculty of Law (no less — law being perhaps the least mutable domain of language use) had written: 'In order to unite the people under a single language tied in with their common culture it was essential that Swahili should become the national language in *every* aspect of national life' (Weston, 1965; my emphasis).

Collapse of English as effective medium

The period from the mid-1960s to the mid-1980s, during which the shift in status of English in Tanzania from second towards foreign language has been taking place, has also witnessed a decline in standards of English in the educational system so severe that, if not arrested, English might soon cease to be a viable medium of education.

The present standard of English

The most recent, and the most systematic, account of present standards of English is contained in a Report prepared for the Tanzanian Ministry of Education and the British Overseas Development Administration (Criper & Dodd, 1984). On the basis of a graded cloze proficiency test which was administered to 2,410 pupils at all levels of the educational system the authors made the following observations:

> Throughout their secondary careers little or no other subject information [i.e. apart from English] is getting across to about 50% of the pupils in our sample. Only about 10% of Form IVs are at a level at which one might expect English medium education to *begin*. (p. 14)

> Only a handful of pupils are at a level adequate for English medium education — 1% of Form I, and the same figure for Form IV. (p. 25)

> The proportion of [Form V] pupils at level 'A' (nearing but not at independent reading level) is still small — 17%. (p. 14)

> [University] students' level of English is substantially below that required for university English medium study. (p. 15) Less than 20% of the sample tested were at a level where they would find it easy to read even the simpler books required for their academic studies. (p. 43)

The current average level of those qualifying to teach, while higher
than the level of those they will teach, is not very much higher. (p. 15)
Though many people concerned with education in Tanzania at present
would probably respond to these statements with dismay, they might well
not find them particularly surprising, since the figures given, though chilling
enough, do little more than provide a hitherto lacking exactness to the
quantification of a state of affairs that has for long, and by many, been
observed, described and bemoaned (e.g. Mlama & Matteru, 1978; Hill,
1980, *inter alia*).

Causes and effects

These are not always easily distinguishable. Declining standards, for
example, are a consequence of the L2–FL shift and, in their turn, a further
impetus to its eventual completion. Broadly, however, the principal causes
of the present low level of English, specifically at the secondary level, may
be grouped as follows: first, the low level of achievement at primary level.
(For a summary of reasons for this see Hill, 1980, based on Trappes-Lomax,
1978.) Second, difficulties in the way of remedying this at secondary level,
associated with (a) lack of learner exposure to English except in class, 'the
actual amount of English that pupils in Form I to IV are exposed to [being]
more similar to the situation occurring in countries where English is being
taught as a foreign language rather than as a medium of instruction or as a
second language' (Criper & Dodd, p. 35); (b) levels of linguistic and
methodological competence of many teachers — though, at secondary
level, by no means all — being insufficient to cope with the overwhelming
difficulties of the situation, this in turn having a depressing effect on morale;
and (c) shortages and other deficiencies of materials.

A third cause is the apparently short, but in fact indefinitely long, life
expectancy of English as medium. For almost 20 years, it has been national
policy to replace English by Swahili medium at all educational levels.
Reaffirmations of this policy, and plans for its implementation, have been
made at more or less regular intervals — 1969, 1970, 1974, 1979, 1982 — the
latest of these being contained in the Report of the Recommendations of
the Presidential Commission on Education (sec. 4.131). This proposed 1985
and 1992 for, respectively, the initiation and completion of the changeover,
the object being: 'to enable as many people as possible to pursue their
studies beyond the primary level without the obstruction of a foreign
language' (p. 209: my translation). A decade or so previously, 'the most
optimistic projections expect that by 1973 all subjects will be taught through

the medium of Swahili up to School Certificate level. This seems very unlikely, but certainly by about 1976 nearly all pre-Form IV teaching will be in Swahili' (Mbunda *et al.*, 1980, written much earlier). The consequence of this prolonged vacillation — a classic case, indeed, of Whiteley's 'conflicting claims of authenticity and modernity' — has been to drain all attempts to do something about English (or language in education generally) of any lasting vigour. There has been stability of a sort, but the debilitating stability of tendencies in unresolved opposition, not that of languages in a harmonious state of functional complementarity.

As to educational effects, the decline in standards of English has, in many secondary schools, resulted almost in the extinction of the language as a living medium. (The situation at senior secondary and university levels is, for various reasons, generally less serious than this.) Both degree of use and degree of usefulness have been affected. With respect to the former, the prediction, quoted above, that Swahili would certainly take over from English at secondary level has, some years later than expected, come true, but in a way that was certainly not expected at the time:

> A mixture [of English and Swahili] is almost universally used, the only exception being schools where the headmaster is consciously and actively trying to ensure that English is used for all purposes through-out the school. In other schools, we estimate that perhaps up to 75% of teaching, at any rate in Form I, is being done through Swahili. (Criper & Dodd, p. 34)

As for degree of usefulness, were it not for the use of Swahili, 'it is hard to see how any genuine education could take place at secondary level' (Criper & Dodd, p. 16). The research of Mlama & Matteru (1978) showed plainly that pupils did not understand their subjects as they should, could express themselves adequately in neither speech nor writing, and indeed were unable, many of them, to participate in an English medium lesson at all, avoiding the eye of the teacher if a question were asked in English (but rushing to put up their hands, and producing an intelligent answer, if the same question were repeated in Swahili). Mlama and Matteru unequivo-cally concluded that the time had come for the medium of education to be (officially) changed. This has not, however, been the decision of the Tanzanian government.

Remedial measures

Notwithstanding the recommendation of the Commission on Education (quoted above) the government has indicated that the medium of education at secondary and tertiary levels will continue to be English. It follows that English medium has to be rehabilitated and, from this, that standards of English must drastically and speedily be raised. The Criper–Dodd Report contains proposals (accepted by the government) for achieving these ends:

1. to introduce throughout the secondary system (Forms I to IV) a graded extensive reading scheme;
2. to produce and implement a six-month immersion programme for the beginning of Form I, as a way of introducing English into subject teaching at an early stage;
3. to stimulate the use of English in the out-of-class school environment;
4. to foster extra-curricular activities involving the use of English.

The rationale behind all of these proposals appears to be the same: that the only way of restoring English at secondary school to 'a level at which it could be properly used as a medium of instruction' is for pupils to receive 'a massive increase in their exposure to English and their use of English' (Criper & Dodd). Mlama & Matteru (1978: 31), in considering the option of taking remedial measures, observe that 'though it is thought that using English as medium helps students to know more English, investigation shows that this is not so' (my translation). The Criper–Dodd proposals, however, clearly go beyond this minimal remedy, both qualitatively and quantitatively. They can be summarised as an attempt to provide 'more formal instruction' (i.e. more of it) — especially in proposals (1) and (2) — and 'other measures' — especially in (3) and (4) — 'compensating for the lack of environmental support' which is characteristic of foreign language as opposed to second language learning situations (Stern, 1983: 16). Whether the measures will suffice for the achievement of the stated objectives is a matter about which, provided we are prepared to be patient, we do not really need to speculate. The answer will be known in a few years' time.

Conclusion

A foreign language — i.e. a non-indigenous language which is not used, outside the classroom, for day to day communication within the speech community — lacks the subjective characteristics requisite for viability as a national medium of education. Over the past two decades, English in Tanzania has, to a significant extent but not yet wholly, acquired the characteristics of a foreign language. During the same period a very marked and serious decline in standards of its use may be attributable to non-linguistic causes, indeed to causes outside the educational system altogether. But other causes, in particular the insufficiency of learners' exposure to the language, and the long unresolved issue of the choice of medium of instruction, are plausibly subsumed under what has been suggested as being the major, overarching, cause — the change of status. The nature of the present proposals to rehabilitate English as medium of education — they amount to a compensatory scheme, designed to give second-language features to a foreign language situation — gives support to this analysis.

References

BRUMFIT, C.J. and ROBERTS, J.T. 1983, *An Introduction to Language and Language Teaching.* London: Batsford.

BULL, W.E. 1964, The use of vernacular languages in education. In D. HYMES (ed.) *Language in Culture and Society.* New York: Harper & Row.

BURT, M. and DULAY, H. 1981, Optimal language learning environments. In J.E. ALATIS *et al.* (eds) *The Second Language Classroom.* Oxford: Oxford University Press.

CRIPER, C. and DODD, W. 1984, *Report on the Teaching of the English Language and its Use as a Medium in Education in Tanzania.* Dar es Salaam: The British Council.

CRIPER, C. and WIDDOWSON, H.G. 1975, Sociolinguistics and language teaching. In J.B.P. ALLEN and S.P. CORDER (eds) *Papers in Applied Linguistics.* London: Oxford University Press.

GORMAN, T. 1971, Sociolinguistic implications of a choice of media of instruction. In W.H. WHITELEY (ed.) *Language Use and Social Change.* Oxford: Oxford University Press.

HILL, C.P. 1980, Some developments in language and education in Tanzania since 1969. In E.C. POLOMÉ and C.P. HILL (eds) *Language in Tanzania.* Oxford: Oxford University Press.

JAMHURI YA MUUNGANO WA TANZANIA 1982, *Mfumo wa elimu ya Tanzania 1981–2000.* Ripoti na mapendekezo ya Tume ya Rais ya Elimu.

LE PAGE, R. 1964, *The National Language Question.* London: Oxford University Press.

MBUNDA, F., BRUMFIT, C.J., CONSTABLE, D. and HILL, C.P. 1980, Language teaching in secondary schools. In E.C. POLOMÉ and C.P. HILL (eds) *Language in Tanzania.* Oxford: Oxford University Press.

MLAMA, P. and MATTERU, M.L. 1978, *Haja ya kutumia Kiswahili kufundishia katika elimu ya juu.* Dar es Salaam: BAKITA.

MOHAMED, W.A. 1975, *The Introduction of Kiswahili as a Medium of Instruction in Tanzanian Secondary Schools: A Diagnostic and Evaluative Study.* MA dissertation, University of Dar es Salaam.

NIDA, E.A. and WONDERLY, W.L. 1971, Communication roles of languages in multilingual societies. In W. WHITELEY (ed.) *Language Use and Social Change.* Oxford: Oxford University Press.

POLOMÉ, E.C. and HILL, C.P. (eds) 1980, *Language in Tanzania.* Oxford: Oxford University Press.

RUBIN, J. and JERNUDD, B.H. 1971, *Can Language be Planned?* The University Press of Hawaii.

STERN, H.H. 1983, *Fundamental Concepts of Language Teaching.* Oxford: Oxford University Press.

TRAPPES-LOMAX, H.R. 1978, English Language Teaching in Tanzania: A Colloquium (Mimeo). University of Dar es Salaam.

WESTON, A.B. 1965, Law in Swahili — Problems in developing the national language. *Swahili* 35, 2.

WHITELEY, W.H. 1971, Some factors affecting language policies in Eastern Africa. In J. RUBIN and B.H. JERNUDD (eds) *Can Language be Planned?* The University Press of Hawaii.

10 The communication skills unit and the language problem at the university of Dar es Salaam

J.M. RUGEMALIRA

Introduction

The discussion of the language problem at Tanzania's post-secondary educational institutions often seems to assume that this is a recent development. The problem that students have in communicating effectively in English is attributed to the development of Swahili and as such it is regarded as having hardly any parallels beyond Tanzania.

However, misgivings about learners' level of proficiency in a medium of education other than their mother tongue have been internationally acknowledged for a long time now. In 1961, for instance, Denny (1963: 50) wrote that

> the general feeling of educationists . . . is that competence in the national or educational language is inadequate and that students are handicapped . . . two university colleges (Nairobi and Addis Ababa) prescribe courses in the medium of instruction as compulsory for all students . . . at Salisbury students whose proficiency is found to be inadequate are 'advised or required' to attend English Proficiency Classes.

Today similar arrangements exist in many universities and colleges across Africa and beyond. There is, for example, a Communication Skills Centre at the University of Zimbabwe, a Language and Study Skills Unit at Nairobi University, and a Communication Skills Unit at the University of Dar es Salaam. Each of these institutions is entrusted with the task of tackling the 'language problem'. But what is the nature of this problem? This chapter critically examines the theoretical answer as well as the practical remedy developed by the Communication Skills Unit (CSU) at the University of Dar es Salaam.

Diagnosis

The CSU was established in 1978 as a semi-autonomous section of the Department of Foreign Languages and Linguistics. It was the University's response to recurrent complaints from a number of lecturers and external examiners that the students were failing to express themselves effectively in English. This failure was deemed to have adverse effects on the students' academic work. The CSU was therefore charged with the task of helping the students to learn more efficiently through the medium of English.

The same year that saw the establishment of the CSU also witnessed the birth of the University Teaching and Learning Improvement Programme (UTLIP) charged with monitoring the quality of teaching and learning within the university. There had been suggestions that the CSU be established as part of UTLIP, but these had been rejected. And this was a significant decision in determining the status of the Unit: it was not going to be a 'remedial service unit' but a full-fledged academic unit teaching regular credit courses and engaged in research.

It was incumbent upon the CSU to determine the nature and extent of the language problem at the university before designing and implementing a solution. For this purpose CSU staff examined students' writing, administered questionnaires to students, interviewed teaching staff across the university faculties, and consulted external examiners' reports.[1] A major conclusion of this investigation was that students' inadequacies manifested themselves at two main levels, *viz.* (a) 'the level of grammatical competence (syntax and lexis at sentence level)' and (b) 'the level of communicative competence (discourse skills)' (Rea, 1980: 50). Subsequently the CSU decided to concentrate on (b) rather than (a), maintaining that the 'majority' of students did not have 'severe inadequacies at the level of grammatical competence' (Rea, 1980: 50). The discourse skills envisaged under (b) include the 'organisation of material in essay writing, presentation of facts and arguments in an orderly fashion, style in academic writing [and] appropriate reading strategies' (cf. Numi & Mcha, 1986: 8).

The above distinction between grammatical competence and communicative competence is rather tenuous. For the appropriate choice of structures and lexical items is part and parcel of the ability to communicate effectively, of what it means to know a language. As Hymes puts it, 'there are several sectors of communicative competence, of which the grammatical is one' (Hymes, 1971: 18). Perhaps the CSU stance is partly a result of the general disenchantment with grammar and the rise of the communicative approach as the dominant fashion in language teaching during the 1970s. The focus was on 'the problem of the student who may be structurally competent, but who cannot communicate effectively' (Johnson, 1979: 192). It is against such a background that the CSU could declare that grammar was not a majority problem. But an examination of the evidence could lead to a different conclusion.

In order to identify students with serious problems in grammar the CSU administers a relatively elementary test — the University Screening Test (UST) — to all first-year students at the beginning of the academic year. Table 10.1 shows the UST results for 1985, 1986 and 1987. The total number of candidates who sat for the test in each year is shown in column 2. Columns 3 to 7 show the distribution of the candidates into different bands of scores. For instance, column 5 shows that, in 1985, 484 candidates, or 57.6% of the total, scored less than 70% on the test. Column 8 shows the number of candidates recommended for the Intensive Grammar Programme (IGP). CSU policy is that any candidate scoring 54% or less on the UST is 'at risk' and should be recommended for the IGP. In practice fewer candidates are recommended due to staff constraints. A comparison of columns 7 and 8 bears this out. This gap between the ideal and reality was widest in 1987 when 24.7% failed, but only 14.3% were recommended.

TABLE 10.1 *UST results*

| Year | UST candidates (total) | 80–100 | Percentage score | | | | IGP |
			79 or less	69 or less	59 or less	54 or less	
1985: N	840	151	689	484	348	236	214
%	100	17.9	82	57.6	41.4	28	25.4
1986: N	596	103	493	363	228	166	159
%	100	17.2	82.7	60.9	38.2	27.8	26.6
1987: N	703	137	566	385	232	174	101
%	100	19.4	80.5	54.7	33	24.7	14.3

Source: UST and IGP files

Using the UST results to determine the extent of the linguistic problem can be controversial. The crucial indicator is what one takes as the passmark.[2] With a passmark of 55% only about a quarter of the students fail (cf. column 7). However, considering the nature of this test, a more realistic passmark should be 70%. With this criterion grammar becomes a majority problem. Column 5 shows that more than half of the candidates fall below this point: 57.6%, 60.9% and 54.7% in 1985, 1986 and 1987 respectively. Criper & Dodd (1984) paint an equally bleak picture:

> [University] students' level of English is substantially below that required for university English medium study. (p. 15)

> . . . less than 20% of the [University] sample tested were at a level where they would find it easy to read even the simpler books required for their academic studies. (p. 43)

These findings could be dismissed as exaggerated and alarmist. It could be pointed out that after all the majority of students (perhaps more than 90%) do manage to complete their studies successfully, and that not all failures can be blamed on the language problem. Put succinctly, the question is this: if the language problem is so serious how do students manage to get their degrees?

One possible reply would maintain that the standards of education have 'fallen' with the standards of English. According to this view, the university is currently producing lower quality graduates than it did in the early years of its existence when a pass in English would have been a condition for admission. Perhaps a similar condition today might exclude all candidates failing to score 70% on the UST. But a comparison of education standards across different periods is a risky business. Moreover, such a nostalgic approach is not wholly justified in view of the fact that the language problem across the universities in Africa is as old as the universities themselves. The issue is certainly much more complex.

The CSU has expressed concern about students who fail to produce 'even a single correct sentence in communication skills courses' but 'manage to pass their other courses which include essay writing in their exams' (CSU meeting, 14.3.1986). There is indeed no clear relationship between students' performance on the UST and their performance in the university examinations. The majority of students identified as being at risk do quite well in the examinations. Probably the largest single factor for this situation is the high level of teachers' tolerance of students' errors. If some lecturers complain about the students' inability to express themselves effectively in English, there are still many others who would say that they look for the content and ignore the poor form of expression. A similar attitude among university staff at Malawi University has been reported by Dede Kamkondo (1987: 9): 'Our students did not need the Queen's English in order to facilitate communication. (If they could communicate in "broken" English why bother?)'

The foregoing discussion would seem to call into question the strong claim that students are put 'at risk' on account of a language problem. A weaker claim might be that students attain a lower performance than they would otherwise be capable of if they did not have a language problem. A variation of that would be that learning is made a little more difficult by the language problem. An appropriate response to the problem posed by the weak claim is to offer a service course to ease learning difficulties and thereby raise performance. The strong claim, on the other hand, requires a rescue operation to save a sinking boat. The CSU was established on the basis of the strong claim, but traces of the weak claim have always been present.

This discussion has raised two questions regarding the language problem at the University of Dar es Salaam. The first is whether or not the problem is essentially one of grammar. The second question concerns the extent of the problem: what proportion of the students are affected and how seriously? The CSU maintains that only a minority of students have severe inadequacies at the level of grammar, but that the majority have problems at the higher level of discourse and study skills. I have, however, suggested that the students' problems in basic grammar are much more serious than the CSU diagnosis indicates.

The Prescription

Following upon its diagnosis of the problem the CSU prescribed two types of courses. The first type consisted of a remedial course in basic English grammar, known as the Intensive Grammar Programme (IGP). The second type consisted of a set of study skills courses designed for specific faculties.

The IGP is meant for those students identified by the UST as being 'at risk'. It is a ten-week course covering ten major topics in grammar (see Appendix A), and is largely self-instructional. The coursebook (developed by the CSU) contains explanations and exercises on each topic. The students read the explanations, do the exercises, and hand in the books for marking. They then meet the tutor in groups for one hour to discuss the week's work.

Relative to the other courses of the CSU the IGP is not considered to be a major preoccupation of the Unit. Student attendance is largely optional even when a student has been recommended to register for the course.[3] Performance on the course is of no consequence. All this is in line with the CSU decision that the language problem at the University is not primarily grammatical; consequently there is a tendency to give the IGP minimal attention. It has been characterised as 'not the most academically rewarding course to teach [even though] it definitely answers a need felt by students themselves' (CSU, 'IGP Course Report 1984', p. 7).

It is doubtful how effective the IGP is in fulfilling the 'need felt by students'. Already in 1982 it was noted that 'these students, some of whom are probably weak in their other subjects, are being asked to do extra work on top of an already heavy workload, and that therefore we cannot expect the IGP course to act as a miracle cure for their language problems' (CSU, 'IGP Course Report 1982'). Attempts to monitor improvement have not been yielding conclusive results mainly because the post-test has always been different from the pre-test (UST), thus rendering the results incomparable. The general impression, though, seems to be that of only modest improvement for some candidates and none for others (cf. IGP reports for 1985 and 1986).

Besides considerations of a heavy workload, it could be argued that the IGP underestimates the task of learning a language by assuming that in ten weeks students can acquire a mastery of the basic English structures, largely by self-instruction. This calls into question the suitability of this particular course. However, a more fundamental question is whether there can be a 'right course' for these learners. It is a question of how effective a remedial language course can be. I shall return to this question later.

CSU resources are mainly directed at the faculty-specific courses, namely the communication skills courses for the faculties of Arts and Social Sciences, Commerce and Management, Engineering, Law, Medicine and Science. Relative to the IGP these courses are regarded as the real business of the unit. Whereas the IGP is an optional, non-credit course for a minority of students, the other courses are largely compulsory and in some cases creditable. They are compulsory in the faculties of Engineering, Law and Medicine. In the Faculty of Arts and Social Sciences, the communication skills course is compulsory only for education students. In the faculties of Commerce and Management and of Science the courses are compulsory for students who fail a faculty-specific proficiency test. The courses are creditable in the faculties of Arts and Social Sciences, Law, and Science.

Communication skills courses do not set out to teach English; rather, they assume that students have an adequate mastery of English. What they seek to do is to teach students how to study efficiently, hence they are also known as study skills courses. The major skills include note-taking, summarising, reading strategies, reference skills and organisation of writing (see Appendix B). Although the courses are quite similar with respect to the skills they deal with, there is considerable variation in the amount of time available for each course. At one extreme is the course for engineering students with only 15 hours available; at the other end, the Arts and Social Sciences course has 60 hours at its disposal. The course for Commerce and Management stands in between, with 40 hours available. Such variations are reflected in the modes of teaching adopted by different courses and in the amount of practice allowed on individual skills. For instance, the course for engineers employs the lecture mode to transmit information to a class of about 180 students. Only a few of the hours are allocated to tutorial sessions in smaller groups of about 20. In contrast to this, in the Arts and Social Sciences course *all* work is done in tutorial groups of about 20 students. And while in this course a topic such as note-taking consists of 10 tasks spread over four to six hours, in the course for engineers the same topic is dealt with in a one-hour lecture and a one-hour tutorial during which only three tasks are performed.

Another significant variation within the courses concerns the choice of resource materials. Each course seeks to teach the various skills with specific reference to the students' academic subjects. The courses draw on authentic texts from the fields of study within each faculty. The concern for authenticity is partly based on intuitive appeal — that a student of engineering will find a text about concrete structures more interesting than one about class struggle — and also on ease of skill transfer. 'By concentrating on the salient features of such authentic texts, we may expect that the course will adequately reflect the particular ordering of skills typically required for processing information within each field of study' (Rea, 1980: 81).

These variations notwithstanding, however, the courses share the basic assumption that students possess an adequate command of English. This was clearly expressed in a handout introducing the communication skills course (CL100) for Arts and Social Sciences to first-year students:

> It is true that most university entrants have an adequate command of English grammar. In fact, some may have been using English in their previous job, and perhaps even teaching English. However, university work places considerable demands on a student's language ability. Grasping the conceptual content of an advanced textbook or lecture, or presenting a relevant and coherent academic essay, is not at all simple. Indeed, even students whose native language is English face problems in adjusting to academic communication. It represents a highly sophisticated level of language use, far above that of mere

grammatical accuracy. CL 100, therefore, is not directly concerned with improving English grammar, but with *developing more advanced and specialised communication skills for academic study.* (Rea, n.d.) In view of the evidence furnished by the UST this comparison of the University of Dar es Salaam students' level of English to that of 'students whose native language is English' is, to say the least, unrealistic.[4] Granted that 'mere grammatical accuracy' is not enough, it should be asked whether the other skills can be taught and learnt if this foundation is shaky or missing. If a student cannot produce 'a single correct sentence' how effectively can he be taught to connect sentences and paragraphs, or construct an argument?

Further Considerations on the Prescription

In order to gain a better understanding of the prescription we need to consider the nature of the task given to the CSU, *viz.,* to run a remedial language course. This is a daunting task in view of considerations of (a) what is achievable by such a course and (b) the general acceptability of the course.

Considerations of what is *achievable* are twofold. First, among the candidates admitted to the university there will be a group whose English has fossilised (Selinker, 1974) at some very early stage in the learning process and who therefore manifest an irremediable mismatch between their level of knowledge of the language and the level demanded by university studies. In this connection it is worth asking whether the group scoring below 55% on the UST can be helped at all. Second, even when a group that could benefit from remedial treatment has been identified, we need to consider the nature of the remedial treatment required. The usual practice is to re-teach what the learners have been exposed to for years. Corder's observation is pertinent: '. . . very often, a lot of work (of this sort) produces little improvement. After all, if the first teaching did not produce the required results, there is no obvious reason why the second teaching should do so (unless the first teaching was too hurried)' (Corder, 1981: 52).

But suppose the first teaching was indeed too hurried or was poorly done, could any remedial programme make good the damage? Fisher (1966) is very optimistic about the possibility of breaking poor linguistic habits and making correct sentence patterns automatic. Although his chief concern is to demonstrate the superiority of what he calls the 'oral pattern practice method' over the 'traditional workbook and grammatical methods' in remedial teaching, his work raises the basic concerns with time and motivation.

As regards time, Fisher notes that although his experimental group recorded significant improvement after remedial treatment, 'it was felt that lessons could have been more than doubly effective had there been twice the number of hours devoted to them' (Fisher, 1966: 54). Fisher further suggests that for better results the remedial course should be taught in secondary school for a full year. As regards motivation and ability to sustain long periods of continuous work, Fisher seems a bit too generous in assessing his subjects. He claims that 'there was certainly no boredom, and both the teacher and the students felt that returns were sustained' (Fisher, 1966: 54). But even if this were true of Fisher's experimental group of 22 students, it is doubtful that the assessment could be generalised to other learners in different situations.

The time constraint has certainly raised questions about how much can be achieved by CSU courses. The 1982 report of the course for engineering students noted that the course had

> reached the limits of its exploitability. The present mix of lectures and tutorials is perhaps the best solution available given the severe time constraints. However, it should be recognized by the Faculty that given the nature of the course and the limitations it labours under, substantial improvements in the study and language skills of the first year students are unlikely (p. 7).

And more recently the external examiner noted that although some courses were already 60 hours in length, it was obvious that students who managed a bare pass were in need of even longer and more intensive courses (cf. McGinley, 1986). It is in view of such observations that some CSU staff members have suggested that students follow a three-month intensive English course before embarking on university studies proper. There is no doubt that such a course would require a tremendous increase in CSU resources, especially manpower, besides entailing logistical problems for the University generally.

Considerations of *acceptability* become particularly relevant because a remedial course is designed to make up for deficiencies in the learner's knowledge of the language. These deficiencies may be due to the learner's failure to grasp the required matter at the relevant stage, or they may be due to lack of exposure to that matter. In such circumstances a remedial course is not likely to be popular: the learner is reminded of his failure and/or deprivation. The teacher, on the other hand, sees himself as teaching matter that ought to be/is dealt with at earlier levels. In other words, a university lecturer would not like to see himself do the work of a secondary school teacher. This would seem to explain the CSU concern for the respectability and acceptability of its courses. The decision to offer credit courses available to all first-year students is to be seen in this context. The approach seems to have evolved like this: the CSU must be accorded appropriate status for the success of its courses (Rea, 1980: 52). A remedial programme appears to be an extension of work covered in the schools and reminds the learner of having failed to grasp the required matter (p. 54). The most acceptable solution, then, is to declare that actually 'only a few' need such a remedial course anyway, while 'all' students can benefit from a study skills course (p. 55). As Rea put it, 'the CSU was anxious not to cut the image of a "remedial" service unit' (p. 55).[5]

The CSU aimed at attracting two different categories of student: those *opting* for a course, and those *referred* by subject lecturers. The major concern here was that the courses should not be regarded as merely courses for the weak students. However, it appears that very few students opted for the CSU course in its first year of operation. So it was decided to make the Arts and Social Sciences course compulsory for all education students in the faculty from the 1979/80 academic year. In this way there was a guaranteed audience.[6]

The foregoing picture of the evolution of CSU courses needs to be complemented by a consideration of the influence exerted by the Unit's clients, *viz.* the various university faculties. Although it is possible to come across individual lecturers who regarded the work of the Unit as irrelevant and misplaced, generally the various faculties had, and still have, fantastic illusions about what the Unit can do or should be doing. The official conception of the problem is something like this: 'The students cannot speak and write proper English. So teach them the language!' In all faculties CSU courses are compulsory either for all first-year students or for a section of these. And the courses are regarded as English language courses. It is worth noting, for instance, that while CSU tutors would not expect students to speak and write better English as a result of having done the CSU course for engineering students, the First Year convenor for the Faculty of Engineering (1984/85) expected the course to improve the students' level of English, particularly grammar (Dr S. Mosha, personal communication). There is thus a mismatch between the CSU's conception of its work and the clients' conception of the Unit's work. In this regard it would be mere wishful thinking if CSU staff thought they could improve the English of 180 engineering students in the 15 hours allocated to the communication skills course.

Outcome and Prognosis

Has the CSU had any impact, then? In 1984 the external examiner for Communication Skills had this to say:

On the matter of the students' general level of performance, I feel that there is still some evidence . . . that despite the best efforts of the CSU, a number of students may not have yet achieved a sufficiently deep-seated mastery of the language and study skills they increasingly need as they progress in their academic studies.
(Waters, 1984)

Two other external examiners expressed a similar view in 1986 and 1987 (cf. reports by McGinley and Hirst). This assessment is particularly disconcerting because it is based on students' performance on examinations set by the CSU itself. It has been noted that even though almost all students doing communication skills courses for credit do pass, a substantial proportion do so on the strength of coursework assessment while failing the final examination itself. This is possible because coursework is heavily weighted in the final grading (60% coursework, 40% examination), and it is in coursework assignments that students get plenty of help from both tutors and fellow students. It has further been noted that only the very best students demonstrate mastery of the communication and study skills taught in the 'regular' communication skills courses. The majority of students, however, lack the basic sentence-level language skills assumed by these courses, and this impairs communication (cf. Hirst, 1987).

Can the CSU have any significant impact? A 1986 report had this answer:

If there is no control of students' proficiency in English and communication skills when they are admitted to the university, there is little more CSU can do to improve matters beyond what it is doing in the present restricted circumstances. As such, improvement is more a matter of policy than pedagogy. (CSU, 1986b: 9)

The report does not indicate the kind of policy envisaged. The options might include allowing more time for CSU courses (e.g. a three-month intensive course), instituting a university entrance examination in English, consolidating the teaching of English in the secondary schools, and switching to Swahili as medium of instruction. Indeed, in view of the prevailing sociolinguistic situation the latter alternative would seem to be the most realistic. It puts into focus the more fundamental question of the medium of education in Tanzania. English has ceased to be an effective medium of learning and teaching in Tanzania's educational system. If anything could

restore English to that position it is most unlikely that CSU-type organs
could be that thing (cf. Rugemalira *et al.*, this volume).

A final question that needs to be asked is 'Whither CSU?'. In her
foreword to the *Proceedings of CSU 'Review Week' Seminar* (CSU, 1985a)
Mcha described the first six years of the CSU (1978–84) as the 'development
stage'. From 1984/85 the Unit entered a 'new stage of consolidation'. The
foregoing discussion seems to call for a reassessment of this view of CSU
history. It would seem that instead of consolidating the *status quo,* the CSU
should seek to determine the effectiveness of its prescription and perhaps
try another formula. Such a formula should adopt a wider perspective on
the problem by seeking to develop the means for tackling it at pre-university
levels.

This shift in focus would require a transformation of the CSU and the
English section in the Department of Foreign Languages and Linguistics into
a Centre for Teaching English as a Foreign Language. The major concerns of
such a centre might include training teachers of English, developing English
teaching materials for various levels and researching into methods of English
Language Teaching. The centre could also offer certificate courses in
English, develop standard tests for certification, and mount specialist
courses in writing, public speaking and translation for the very best students.

Endowed with the largest single concentration of English language
experts in Tanzania, the CSU ought to investigate these wider avenues of
contributing to the teaching and learning of English in the country. There is
no doubt that these challenges would be more academically rewarding for
staff than a course like the IGP, besides pre-empting worries about
presenting the image of a remedial service unit.

Epilogue

The situation in Tanzania, and of the CSU in particular, is not unique.
Experience from Malawi and Zimbabwe, where English occupies a more
prestigious position than in Tanzania, indicates that remedial courses at
tertiary institutions are no more effective or acceptable. This implies that
efforts for tackling language proficiency problems should be focused at the
early levels of learning the languages in question so that a good foundation
can be established. And in many African countries it should be possible to
plan for the eventual replacement of a foreign language with a local
language; but for as long as English, French and Portuguese remain the
languages of education in African schools and universities, then the
'language problem' will always be with us.

Notes to Chapter 10

1. Much of the information related to this needs assessment exercise is documented in volumes 1 and 2 of *Language for Education* (Communication Skills Unit, 1980/1983).

2. In order to promote the acceptability of its courses, the CSU avoids use of the terms 'passmark' and 'fail' preferring 'cut off point' and 'at risk'.

3. Only recently the Faculty of Arts and Social Sciences ruled that the IGP be compulsory for students registered in that faculty and recommended by the CSU to do the IGP.

4. In this connection if Swahili were the medium of education, a communication skills course in Swahili would be justified in assuming that students have an adequate command of the language.

5. A similar uneasiness with respect to 'remedial' work was expressed in a recent paper by A. Love (1987) of the Communication Skills Centre, University of Zimbabwe. Love argues that 'our work is not primarily "remedial" but "developmental"' and that 'it is not a cost-effective use of time to concentrate on problems which may well be "fossilized" and therefore likely to be highly resistant to attention at tertiary level' (p. 1).

6. This arrangement has persisted despite the fact that by all standards education students are no more 'at risk' than the other students; cf. M. Norris, 'Selecting students for communication skills courses in the Arts Faculty' in CSU (1985a), *Proceedings of CSU 'Review Week' Seminar* pp. 107–10.

Appendix A

Intensive Grammar Programme: Contents

Unit 1: *Basic Sentence Structure*
Subjects, verbs and objects
Noun phrase construction
Verb agreement

Unit 2: *The Tense System*
Present and past tenses
Descriptions and reports
Instructions

Unit 3: *Noun Classes*
Countable and uncountable nouns
General statements

Unit 4: *Non-finite Verb Forms*
Verbs used as objects
Verbs after prepositions
Verbs used to describe nouns

Unit 5: *The Use of Articles*
Indefinite reference: 'a'
Specific reference: 'the'

Unit 6: *Verb Phrases*
Verb phrase construction
Questions
Negative statements

Unit 7: *Sentence Connection*
Conjunctions
Pronouns
Relative pronouns

Unit 8: *Passive Verb Forms*
Use of the passive
Use of 'by' and 'with'

Unit 9: *Perfect Verb Forms*
Present perfect
Past perfect
Adverbials of time

Unit 10: *Modal Verbs*
Use of modal verbs
Conditional sentence
'Hypothetical' past tense

Appendix B

Sample of Kinds of Skills Taught in Communication Skills Courses

1. *Note-taking*
    a. Recognising organisation in texts: titles, subtitles, numbering, spacing, indentation, sectioning.
    b. Recognising main points and details: headings, topic sentences, metacomments, (in speech) paralinguistic features, connectors.
    c. Compression of information in notes: abbreviations; symbols; (nonverbal information: charts, graphs, diagrams).
    d. (Expressing) organisation in notes (layout, numbering, spacing, indentation).

2. *Understanding Lectures*

    a. Recognising organisation in lectures: metacomments, paralinguistics, connectors, grammatical cohesion.
    b. Recognising status of the information: metacomments, paralinguistics — voice quality, tempo gestures, grammatical cohesion.

   c. Recognising function of information and meaning relationships: connectors and discourse markers — exemplification, evidence, contrasting, adding, concluding, summarising, reformulating, emphasising.

3. *Interpreting Essay Questions*

   a. Analysing essay questions: recognising key instruction words and special conditions. Instruction words: discuss, describe, analyse, argue, give an account of, why, give reasons. Special condition words: briefly, in the Third World, with the aid of a map.

   b. Distinguishing between fact and opinion:

   Factual essays:
- Describe . . . .
- Give examples of . . . .
- Give an account of . . . .
- Briefly state the . . . .

   Opinion essays:
- What are the arguments? . . . .
- Discuss . . . .
- Give reasons for . . . .
- Justify . . . .

4. *Organisation of Writing*

   a. Planning of written work: outlines and drafts:
- skeletal outlines
- detailed outlines
- preparing drafts

   b. Indicating good organisation, headings, sectioning: introductions, body, conclusion.

   c. Writing introductions; essay structure and organisation.

   d. Expressing meaning relationships:
- grammatical cohesion
- connectors

   e. Expressing status of information:
- connector
- metacomments
- grammatical cohesion

   f. Writing conclusions:
- signal words

5. *Using Sources of Information*

   a. Selecting relevant information: book cover titles, table of contents, index, glossary.
   b. Using the library and reference sources: library author and index catalogues (when compiling bibliography).
   c. Assessing usefulness of a reference/book: index cards.
   d. Compiling a bibliography, bibliographic formats.
   e. Use of citations and quotations: footnotes.
   f. Acknowledging source of information: citations, quotations, footnotes, introductory verbs: argue, state, report, etc.

6. *Reading Strategies*

   a. Setting a purpose for reading.
   b. Recognising main points and details: topic sentences, titles and subtitles, generalisations, example.
   c. Skimming for general information: topic sentences, introductions and conclusions.
   d. Scanning for specific details: tables of contents, glossary, index, titles, sub-titles.
   e. Recognising organisation in a text: sectioning, paragraphing, numbering, layout.
   f. Predicting information: signal words, metacomments.
   g. Making inferences: facts, opinions, generalisations.
   h. Recognising writer's attitude to information: stylistic features and modality.

7. *Reporting Practical Research*

   a. Collecting relevant data: questionnaires, interviews.
   b. Organising data: graphs, tables, diagrams.
   c. Describing data: talking about data:
      — Hypothesis, premise, conclusion, generalisations
      — Words of quantity, frequency and degrees
   d. Organising information: sectioning, paragraphing.
   e. Using appropriate style and register: tenses, reported speech, passive voice.
   f. Expressing attitude to information or data.
   g. Use of non-verbal information: tables, diagrams, graphs, maps, etc.

8. *Presenting an Argument*

  a. Recognising difference between facts and opinions.
  b. Recognising parts of an argument: premise, evidence, conclusion or generalisation.
  c. Expressing an argument: expression of attitude:
     — use of modality
     — use of style and register
     — use of point of view

9. *Oral Presentation*

  a. Introducing a topic.
  b. Maintaining interest of listeners: metacomments, voice quality, tempo, gestures, eye contact, hesitations, gap fillers.
  c. Using appropriate style in oral presentation.
  d. Concluding a discussion.
  e. Handling questions from listeners.
  f. Use of aids.

NB. Oral Presentation forms part of project work. In other courses, e.g. CL 105 and EG 102, Oral Presentation is not done. In CL 100 Oral Presentation is based on topics suggested by specialist tutors, in CL 104 it is based on case studies, while in CL 101 students have to do field or library research.

References

BRUMFIT, C.J. and JOHNSON, K. 1979, *The Communicative Approach to Language Teaching*. Oxford: Oxford University Press.

CORDER, S.P. 1981, *Error Analysis and Interlanguage*. Oxford: Oxford University Press.

CRIPER, C. and DODD, W.A. 1984, *Report on the Teaching of English and its Use as a Medium in Education in Tanzania*. Dar es Salaam: The British Council.

COMMUNICATION SKILLS UNIT 1980/1983, *Language for Education* (vol. 1, 1980; vol. 2, 1983). University of Dar es Salaam.

— 1983, *Intensive Grammar Programme: a Workbook in Basic English Grammar for Academic Purposes*.

— 1985a, *Proceedings of CSU 'Review Week' Seminar, 15–21 March 1985*.

— 1985b, *Writing Skills for Engineering*.

— 1986a, *Communication Skills for Arts and Social Sciences* (Sourcebook and Workbook).

— 1986b, Communication skills for Commerce and Management; Course report for 1985/86.

— Intensive Grammar Programme Course Report 1982.

— Intensive Grammar Programme Course Report 1984.

— Intensive Grammar Programme Course Report 1985/86.
— Intensive Grammar Programme Course Report 1986/87.
DEDE KAMKONDO, W.C. 1987, The Role of a Linguist at an Agricultural College: The case of Bunda College of Agriculture. Paper presented at the conference of the Language Association of SADCC Universities, September 1987.
DENNY, N. 1963, Language and education in Africa. In J. SPENCER (ed.) *Language in Africa*, Papers of the Leverhulme Conference on Universities and the Language Problems of Tropical Africa, held at University College, Ibadan 29.12.1961–6.1.1962, pp. 40–52.
FISHER, J.C. 1966, *Linguistics in Remedial English*. The Hague: Mouton.
HIRST, S. 1987, External Examiners' Report: Communications Skills Unit, Faculty of Arts and Social Sciences, University of Dar es Salaam, Academic Year 1986–87.
HYMES, D. 1971, On communicative competence. In C.J. BRUMFIT and K. JOHNSON (eds) 1979, *The Communicative Approach to Language Teaching*. Oxford: Oxford University Press.
JOHNSON, K. 1979, Communicative approaches and communicative processes. In C.J. BRUMFIT and K. JOHNSON (eds) *The Communicative Approach to Language Teaching*. Oxford: Oxford University Press.
LOVE, A. 1987, Imprecision in the Writing of Science Students. Paper presented at the conference of the Language Association of SADCC Universities, September 1987.
MCGINLEY, K. 1986, External Examiners' Report, Communication Skills Unit, Faculty of Arts and Social Sciences, University of Dar es Salaam, session 1985/86.
NUMI, D.M. and MCHA, Y.Y. 1986, Teaching English for Academic Survival at the Tertiary Level: The Case of the Communication Skills Unit at the University of Dar es Salaam. Paper presented at the Conference on English in East Africa, 24–27 March 1986.
REA, P. 1980, The Communication Skills Unit: 1978–1980. *Language for Education* 1.
— n.d., CL 100: Communication Skills for Arts and Social Sciences. Promotional handout for students, CSU, University of Dar es Salaam.
SELINKER, L. 1974, Interlanguage. In J.C. RICHARDS (ed.) *Error Analysis: Perspectives on Second Language Acquisition*. Essex: Longman.
WATERS, A. 1984, External Examiners' Report: Communication Skills Unit, Faculty of Arts and Social Sciences, University of Dar es Salaam, session 1983/84.

11 Accepted language behaviour as a basis for language teaching: A comparison of English in Kenya and Tanzania[1]

J. SCHMIED

This chapter argues in favour of recognising generally accepted forms of East African English (EAfrE) usage as a target norm in English language teaching, and illustrates the processes involved by comparing developments in Kenya and Tanzania. It summarises the sociolinguistic background, which determines attitudes and acceptability, describes some of the language forms actually used and highlights some of the problems involved in developing a norm for Educated East African English (EdEAfrE) based on accepted language behaviour.

The Sociolinguistic Background

The knowledge and use of languages in East Africa is determined by a complex interplay of language history, policies and attitudes (cf. Gorman, 1971 for Kenya or Schmied, 1985 for Tanzania). The 'trifocal situation' of the international language (English), the supranational language (Kiswahili) and the subnational ethnic, or vernacular, languages are summarised in Figure 11.1. Besides historical determinants in early language spread and in colonial language policy, the differences between the two East African countries are the result of the deliberate expansion of Kiswahili in Tanzania during the last 25 years. For intranational purposes the Tanzanian pattern with an accepted national language (Kiswahili) may be more desirable for a nation-state because it makes it easier for the government to reach the

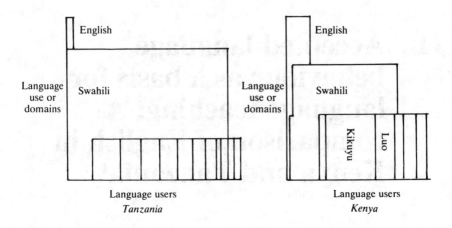

FIGURE 11.1 *Language use and language users in Tanzania and Kenya*

people as well as for the people to participate in national developments. It becomes problematic, however, if a language, as is the case with English in Tanzania, is still used for important functions in certain 'modern sectors' of the country (see below) when access to it through formal education is restricted to a small minority (the English-speaking population is below 5% in Tanzania, but at least three times as large in Kenya).

When we apply the broad categories of English as a Second Language (ESL) and English as an International Language (EIL), we can classify Kenya as an ESL country, since English is used in parliament and government offices, and it is the medium of instruction from upper primary education onwards. Tanzania, on the other hand, can almost be seen as an EIL country nowadays, since English is primarily used in foreigner-related sectors, such as economic co-operation and development and the adoption of scientific and technical ideas from the international scene, and only secondarily in some intranational communication, i.e. in business letters, in medical records, at the high court and in secondary schools as a medium of instruction.

It is worth noting that different sociolinguistic positions also entail important consequences for English language teaching: different emphasis is placed on different language skills (e.g. written and spoken) or on different teaching methods (e.g. communicative approaches are more appropriate in an ESL than in an EIL situation).

Language Behaviour

A closer look at the type of English used in East Africa reveals a wide range of interlanguages which co-vary largely with the socio-educational background of their users. Linguistic factors governing this variation are mother-tongue influence and (over-) generalisation (possibly to different degrees in EIL and ESL countries). Compared to ENL (English as a Native Language) standards (such as 'Educated South-East English English', which is often still regarded as *the* Standard English in Africa) a process of Africanisation (indigenisation or nativisation, cf. Kachru, 1986) of English has taken place. Is this Africanisation the linguistic explanation for the so-called 'declining standards of English'? Although this development has been deplored in many African nations since their independence, it is understandable in view of the Africanisation of the teaching staff and the expansion of education in general during the last 25 years.

This Africanisation of English is most prominent on the level of pronunciation. Generally the lack of quantitative distinctions and of diphthongisation on the phonemic and some intrusive vowels (*i*'s in consonant clusters or nasals before plosives) and the syllable-timed rhythm (with few weak forms) on the supraphonemic level are most obvious features. Figure 11.2 summarises some of these features, the most common vowel and consonant phonemes, quantitatively.

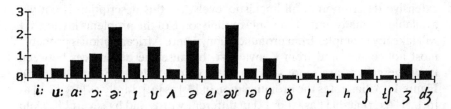

FIGURE 11.2 *'Africanisation' of 21 vowels and consonants in comparison (3 = frequent/extreme, 0 = no differences from Standard English/RP)*

On the lexical level we find some East Africanisms, mainly loan words from Kiswahili, in common use, although their number is certainly limited (about 100). They reflect cultural 'specialities', such as *ngoma* (traditional dance), *ugali* (thick maize porridge) and *duka* (small shop), and political 'specialities', such as *harambee* (self-reliance) in Kenya, *ujamaa* in Tanzania and *wananchi* (fellow-countrymen) in both. Some of these lexemes have even entered Standard English (*askari, baobab, bwana* and *safari* (with semantic specification) can even be found in the Concise Oxford Dictionary). The semantic side is difficult to assess, but certain extensions of meaning (e.g. *arm* for *hand*), confusion of semantically similar lexemes (e.g. *take over–overtake, accept–agree*) and slightly different shades of meaning can be noticed frequently.

Syntactic features are at least noticeable on the morpho-syntactic side, with, compared to British Standard English, the omission of articles, different categorisations of *count* vs. *non-count* nouns, generalisation of question tags ('isn't it') and redundant pronouns (in subject and relative functions). On the 'purely syntactic' side, generalisations are less easy as slight differences of meaning or emphasis may be involved in unconventional word orders, etc. Most of the syntactic features can also be found in other African or 'New' Englishes.

Specific discourse features can also be considered. Some 'ritual' greetings, with an extensive use of 'How are you?' seem to reflect African languages (and of course culture) more than English, whereas other forms reflect rather formal, and even biblical, styles from the old colonial and missionary school tradition in East Africa.

Accepting Language Behaviour

Studies on the acceptability of language behaviour presuppose an extensive description at all linguistic levels. As this description is not yet available for many areas I can only outline some of the problems involved. I will take my examples from pronunciation, where Africanisation is probably most noticeable, and from Kenya first, because the differences between language groups are more striking there (for details see Schmied, 1989). Figure 11.3 illustrates the pronunciation of [ə:] as [a:], rarely as [e:], [ə u] as [o:], [1] as [r] and [ʃ] as [s] or [ʒ] in different words and by several Kenyan groups with different ethnic backgrounds or mother-tongues. It shows that [ə u] and [ə:] are clearly very general features in EAfrE, but whereas [ə u] poses no problems as far as its acceptance is concerned, [ə:] seems more difficult as it merges with other phonemes. Here acceptability and intelligibility are important. Although generally Standard English (even including RP) is still widely considered as the target norm for teaching purposes, many East Africans would shrug off this obvious discrepancy between theoretical norm and actual language behaviour, saying 'I don't want to strain myself so much to say [fə:st] only to sound British' or 'This would seem snobbish to my colleagues'. As far as intelligibility is concerned, the frequent mergers in EAfrE seem to be much less of a problem for East

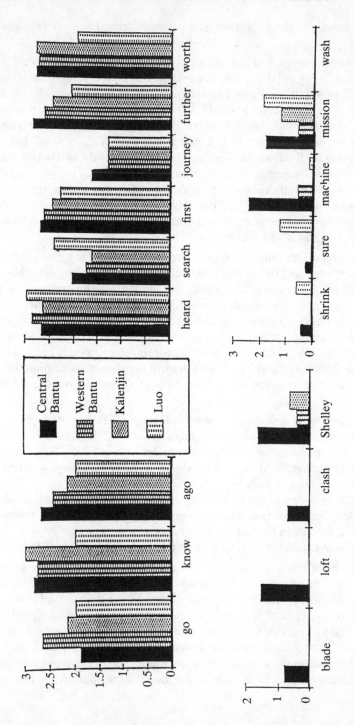

FIGURE 11.3 *The pronunciation of English words containing [əu], [ə:], [l] and [ʃ] by four Kenyan language groups*

Africans themselves than for foreigners unaccustomed to this language behaviour.

With other pronunciation features Africans are less 'generous'. The pronunciation of [1] as [r] is a less consistent, but typical feature of many Bantu speakers. But it is ridiculed and stigmatised, even by those who use it themselves (a typical remark could be: 'You know, we have this *r/l* problem'). Thus although this feature is clearly language behaviour, it is not accepted. Our final example is [ʃ], which is partly, i.e. in word initial position, typical for the Luo (the Western Nilote in general), and partly, i.e. in central position, a more general phenomenon. Thus many people tend to accept 'common' modifications, e.g. a slightly voiced pronunciation, but still stigmatise an initial [ʃ] as [s]. This shows that at the level of pronunciation some more general and consistent features of East African English are recognised and accepted.

At the level of grammar deviations are normally used in a less general and consistent way, and this is why it is even more difficult to analyse them. But the following examples of a small test among teacher trainees may suffice to illustrate that some East African structures are either not recognised as deviant or not marked as wrong (see Schmied, 1988 for details). We take the omission of articles (e.g. definite article in S1 and indefinite article in S2) and plural marking for *non-count* nouns (e.g. in S3 and S4) as relatively salient cases, and the use of adverbs as conjunctions (e.g. in S5 and S6) and lexical redundancy (e.g. in S7 and S8) as more subtle problems:

S1.   Tanzania is now under _ new leadership of Hassan Mwinyi.
S2.   He won by _ overwhelming majority.
S3.   I was in charge of all correspondence*s*.
S4.   The replacement of the headmaster caused some discontent*s* among the teachers.
S5.   The box should not be too big, *also* its weight should be limited.
S6.   *So* to fulfil this task we had to get up very early in the morning.
S7.   His fluency in English *language* was superb.
S8.   The age limit for driving a car should be between 65 and 75 *years*.

The results of this test among two groups of teacher trainees are given in Figure 11.4. This shows that even relatively clear cases of deviation (i.e. where clear English grammar rules exist), such as the omission of articles and the insertion of plural markers after *non-count* nouns, are accepted or not recognised by many Africans. But there are differences in consistency: article omissions are more common deviations than unusual plural markings. With less salient deviations, which are often even in Standard English a matter of feeling and degree, such as questions of the appropriate linking

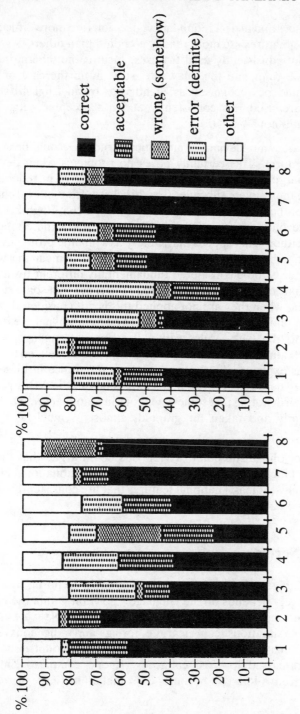

FIGURE 11.4 *Recognising and accepting East African English grammatical constructions (two groups of teacher trainees; $N_1 = 37$, $N_2 = 30$). The horizontal scale corresponds to test items S1 to S8.*

between sentences and lexical redundancy, decisions are more difficult. But even here some features are more readily accepted than others. Again one could argue that consistently used features, such as the 'liberal interpretation' of article rules and the 'play safe' strategy in the case of lexical redundancy could be recognised as Standard African English, whereas features that are used less consistently and not accepted (e.g. double negation), should not.

Thus at least some 'deviant' grammatical structures could be accepted as an African norm. This certainly poses no problems when deviations violate only marginal Standard English tendencies (e.g. in redundancy), and even when they violate sub-rules (e.g. articles in front of post-modified nouns) they can be accepted on the grounds that other English varieties (dialects and second-language 'Englishes') do not follow these tendencies and sub-rules either. This applies particularly as semantic problems do not normally occur in these categories. It does not, of course, mean that African English grammar is to be considered fundamentally different from British English grammar, only that it is simplified in the sense that some sub-rules are optional and when they are not applied this is not considered 'wrong'. Many of these grammatical deviations seem to be *intra*-lingual, i.e. they are more related to the (sub-) rules within the English language, whereas pronunciation features seem to be more *inter*-lingual, i.e. related to the first languages. This explains why there seems little difference in these grammatical features between Kenyan and Tanzanian varieties. But generally speaking it is worth noting that some deviations in grammar seem to be used fairly consistently and taken for granted, almost as much as those in pronunciation.

From a sociolinguistic point of view one could argue that there are several levels of inclusive supranational, national and subnational linguistic features, and only (at least) national features that are consistently used can be accepted as a national norm.

Developing Norms

Whether indigenous forms are accepted as linguistic norms by a speech community largely depends on the language's position within the country. Whereas the norms in the EFL and ENL (English as Native Language/ Mother Tongue) situations seem clear, i.e. foreign and indigenous respectively, they remain a subject of great controversy in ESL countries and have hardly been discussed for EIL countries. If one compares English in Tanzania and Kenya today, it becomes clear that an increasing divergence in English use and proficiency has taken place during the last 25 years. Through the declining use of English for intranational purposes and the decreasing ENL influence (British and American), the deviations from 'Standard English' seem to have increased in Tanzania more than in Kenya. On the other hand, it is obvious that in relation to the position of English in the country and to possible communication partners, applied linguists and teachers could allow more variation and 'deviation' in the ESL country Kenya than in the almost-EIL country Tanzania. If, however, one sees East Africa as a geographical and linguistic unity, it would seem desirable to coordinate the developments. Useful as it may be, even with the new awareness of the importance of English for Tanzania it remains doubtful whether some kind of (planned) supranational harmonisation towards a norm of 'Educated East African English' is possible.

The first step in this direction would be a detailed description of EAfrE usage on all levels, since EAfrE, as I have outlined here, certainly exists as a performance variety distinct from British Standard English. The next step would then be to identify an acceptable level for a standard that would be, on the one hand, sufficiently close to other standards of English to fulfil the linguistic function of communication, and on the other hand sufficiently distinct from them to fulfil the sociolinguistic function of expressing an African identity. As it is, of course, impossible to accept every form of English used in Africa, the establishment of certain norms is necessary in variety development, especially for teaching purposes. English teachers must be given some guidelines to help them 'navigate between permitting the intolerable and attempting the impossible'.

As I have shown above, 'generally accepted language behaviour' could be taken as a guideline for codifying an indigenous norm for East Africa. But this presupposes extensive attitude studies about the acceptability of East African forms, before it can be codified directly in a grammar or usage book of EAfrE or indirectly in Kenyan and Tanzanian school books. Later this codified variety of EdEAfrE could be propagated in the mass media, e.g. in broadcasts by the Voice of Kenya and Radio Tanzania, and used as a guideline for interlanguage corrections. The final aim would be the acceptance and widespread use of this institutionalised variety of English by an educated majority. This projection of national variety development is much more likely to happen in Kenya than in Tanzania, but even there it has hardly begun (cf. the more 'advanced' development of English in Nigeria in Bamgbose, 1982).

In conclusion, I would like to mention briefly some of the advantages that the development of an institutionalised East African English could offer. Compared to the existing 'Educated South Eastern English English' ideal, it is obviously not yet sufficiently codified in usage books, grammars and dictionaries; nevertheless, it is elaborated (with different registers), it has been widely adopted and experienced in use in East Africa, it is under the present circumstances a much more reasonable teaching objective and it may even be accepted — if it is eventually accessible as a codified variety. Consequently, linguists interested in English in East Africa might regard making a contribution towards such a codified variety as an important research goal.

Notes

1. The research project on which this account is based constitutes part of the Africa research programme carried out at the University of Bayreuth (West Germany) under the general title of 'Identity in Africa', which aims at supporting field research and the cooperation between Africans and Europeans. The major issues involved in the English project are discussed in detail in Schmied (1989).

References

BAMGBOSE, A. 1982, Standard Nigerian English: Issues of identification. In B. KACHRU (ed.) *The Other Tongue: English across Cultures*. Urbana: Illinois University Press, pp. 99–111.

GORMAN, T.P. 1971, *A Survey of Educational Language Policy; and an Enquiry into Patterns of Language Use and Levels of Language Attainment among Secondary School Entrants in Kenya*. PhD thesis, University of Nairobi.

KACHRU, B.B. 1986, *The Alchemy of English. The Spread, Functions and Models of Non-Native Englishes*. Oxford: Pergamon Press.

SCHMIED, J. 1985, *Englisch in Tansania. Sozio- und interlinguistische Probleme*. Heidelberg: Groos.

— 1988, Recognizing and accepting East African English grammar. In *The Place of Grammar in the Teaching of English*. International Conference, British Council, Nairobi, April 1988, pp. 94–101.

— 1989, National and subnational features in Kenyan English. In J. CHESHIRE (ed.) *English around the World: Sociolinguistic Perspectives*. Cambridge: Cambridge University Press.

12 Swahili terminological modernisation in the light of the present language policy of Tanzania

H.J.M. MWANSOKO

Introduction

Terminological modernisation becomes necessary once there is a need to treat new topics, especially in professional communication (Ferguson, 1968; Selander, 1980: 22). The adoption of Swahili as the national and official language of independent Tanzania (then Tanganyika) in 1963 and 1967 respectively (Abdulaziz, 1972), undoubtedly increased its prestige and functions. Subsequently, it became the language used to conduct most of the government's (internal) official business, including the Parliament, the language of primary education teaching (with a possibility of extending its use to some post-primary teaching as well), the language of lower courts, etc. (see Morrison, 1976; Khamisi, 1980; Polomé, 1980; Abdulaziz, 1980; Hill, 1980 for details on this issue).

The decision to use Swahili for conducting almost the whole gamut of political and public business and as a medium of education meant that many new Swahili terms had to be introduced into the language to express the concepts which had been hitherto 'unexpressable' in Swahili. As Fishman (1977: 37) has indicated, when a language moves into functions for which it was not previously accepted or employed its modernisation becomes necessary, if it is to be able to fulfil its new roles.

Throughout the 1970s and early 1980s the emphasis of Swahili terminological modernisation was on the preparation of the technical terms needed for post-primary teaching. This was motivated by the government's language policy of the early 1970s which favoured and encouraged the change of the medium of instruction from English to Swahili in post-primary

133

education (Trappes-Lomax, Besha & Mcha, 1982). The switch-over to Swahili-medium policy at post-primary level was, however, officially shelved in 1984 (see the booklet *Educational System in Tanzania Towards the Year 2000: Recommendations of the 1982 Presidential Commission on Education as Approved by the Party and Government*, published by the Ministry of Education in October 1984).

The new post-primary education medium policy has resulted in serious repercussions for terminology work in Swahili. On the one hand, Swahili terminology developers feel that the work they had been doing for the past decade (*viz.* developing terms for post-primary use) seems now to be irrelevant (cf. the Editorial of *Kiswahili* Vol. 52/1 and 52/2, 1985). On the other hand, they are not motivated to continue elaborating more Swahili technical terms 'when [the utilisation] of their work has to wait for some distant decision at some unknown date by some indeterminable person or institution' (Yahya-Othman, this volume).

I wish to argue in this chapter that Swahili terminologists still have much work to do in their field, not only because of the expanding role of Swahili in the other-than-education fields, but also because of the various limitations of the existing Swahili terminologies which need to be solved.

Motivation for Further Terminological Modernisation

There are several reasons why terminology work in Swahili is and will continue to be required. In the first place the ever-expanding use of Swahili in political and public sectors (save most of secondary and tertiary education) means that more and more Swahili terms will be needed to conduct, for example, the Parliament, all political meetings and ideological classes organised by Chama Cha Mapinduzi — CCM, the country's sole political party — as well as administrative and commercial business in almost all public and private institutions. The development of such terms is the responsibility of Swahili terminologists.

Secondly, although the policy of extending Swahili medium to post-primary teaching has now been shelved, strong ideological and educational arguments in favour of Swahili medium in secondary and tertiary education continue to be viewed (see, for example, Rubagumya, 1986; Yahya-Othman, this volume). Such pro-Swahili medium arguments can only be interpreted by terminologists as an indication that the question of post-primary Swahili medium has not been completely abandoned — especially by language experts who are aware (either through their own empirical studies or reference to such studies) that the sociolinguistic situation prevailing in Tanzania still favours the use of Swahili medium at post-primary levels. The change of the education medium policy, therefore, should be taken by terminologists as a challenge to spur them towards ensuring that the drawbacks which necessitated this change in policy (one of which is the lack of adequate and efficient Swahili specialised scientific and technical terms (Polomé, 1979; Rubagumya, 1986)) are alleviated as soon as possible. It should be noted that until now there has been no 'formal' government directive prohibiting further development of Swahili terminologies for post-primary education as a result of the new medium policy. Therefore, further development of such terms is still, at least in theory, envisaged by both the government and the public.

Thirdly, there is a strong indication that Swahili may soon be adopted as a working language of the Organisation of African Unity and regional institutions of East and Central Africa (Temu, 1986). The successful implementation of this decision will, undoubtedly, very much depend on the availability of adequate and efficient Swahili technical terms. In addition, the present situation of terminology work in Swahili, as has been hinted earlier, has various limitations which require the terminologists to look for theoretical and practical solutions to solve them. Let us examine in detail this issue.

Overview of the Present Situation of Terminological Modernisation

Most evaluation studies of terminology work in Swahili (see, for example, Tumbo, 1982; Abdulaziz, 1972; MacWilliam, 1985; Mdee, 1983; Mwansoko, in preparation) indicate that this work is far from being satisfactory. First of all, the number of technical terms available for most of the various fields of learning is very limited. Until 1981, for example, there were only 182 Swahili phonology terms (Gibbe, 1981: 2). Secondly, some of the available technical terms seem to have been haphazardly developed and, therefore, are inconsistent and confusing. Thirdly, the time taken in developing the terms is very long. Furthermore, the dissemination of the officially approved terminology lists is very poor.

The terms are limited in number because the procedure used in their elaboration, namely, 'free term translation' whereby terminology developers first look for the sense of a certain English technical term and seek to identify its equivalent in Swahili, is time-consuming and not very productive quantitatively. For example, by following this method it took the Literature Section of the Institute of Kiswahili Research (IKR) four years to prepare a draft proposal of merely 252 literature terms (see *Final Report on the Literature Terminology Project*, 1983). The translation method is further constrained in that by translating the terms according to alphabetical order, concepts are assigned terms without attempting to preserve their inter-relationships, thereby producing inconsistencies. For instance, in the terms:

> *kilele*   'climax'
> *mpomoko*   'anticlimax'

the concept 'climax' appears to have been rendered inconsistently. In phonetics the nasal stops are called 'nazali' but nose alone is 'pua', cf. *chemba ya pua* 'nasal chamber'. Examples of such inconsistencies are many and can be found in terminology lists of all subjects. Moreover, since the terms are elaborated individually, usually following the users' demands, it is almost impossible to have a fuller coverage of the terms of the various subjects or semantic fields (cf. Ohly & Gibbe, 1982).

Some of the existing Swahili technical terms are inconsistent and confusing because of unclear and contradictory guidelines followed in the course of their elaboration. For example, the National Swahili Council (NSC), which is the highest authority for co-ordinating the implementation of the government's Swahili language policy in Tanzania, has directed that the sources of Swahili terminological modernisation in order of priority are:

a. Swahili itself and its non-standard varieties
b. Bantu languages
c. Other (non-Bantu) African languages
d. Foreign languages (*Kakulu* No. 3, 1982: 15).

The emphasis on greater use of Swahili, its non-standard varieties and other Bantu and non-Bantu languages prior to borrowing from foreign languages can only be interpreted as being based on nationalistic purism because very little lexicographic research into the Swahili non-standard varieties and the other indigenous languages has been done so far (Khamisi, 1986; Dunn, 1985; MacWilliam, 1986) to enable them to be used as productive resources of technical terminologies. In addition, most of these languages (or language varieties), 'are not used in the subjects for which words are sought' (Dunn, 1985: 39).

Although the NSC has directed terminologists to incorporate in Swahili loan terms from foreign languages, the choice of the foreign language(s) on which to base the loans has not yet been clearly stated. Furthermore, no proper guidelines have been set up for adopting and adapting the international foreign terms (Mdee, 1983). The suffix '*-ia*', based on classical Greek '*-logia*', for example, seems to be gaining ground in Swahili for the formation of terms with the concept 'study of'. Thus foreign terms ending in '-ology' and '-ics' have their concept 'study of' rendered by '-ia' in Swahili, for example:

fizikia	'physics'
fonolojia	'phonology'
etimolojia	'etymology'

But at the same time this concept (i.e. 'study of') has also been rendered by *taaluma ya*, lit. 'science of', which is borrowed from Arabic, for example:

taaluma ya fonimu	'phonemics' (Gibbe, 1981: 6)
taaluma ya drama	'dramaturgy' (NSC, 1984)

On the other hand, even the suffix '-ia' is not consistently being used in the terms where it has been decided to apply it. It variously appears as either '-i' or '-a' as is shown in the following examples:

fonetiki	'phonetics'
akustika	'acoustics'
prosodi	'prosody' (Gibbe, 1981)

Thus the adoption of international terms, most of which are borrowed from or via English, is quite haphazard.

The procedure through which the Swahili terms are elaborated and formally approved for use is time-consuming because of the treatment of terminology 'elaboration' and 'standardisation' as two separate processes which can be handled by two different groups of people and at different times. The main reason for separating these processes lies in the NSC's involvement in both language status planning and corpus planning. The actual elaboration of the terms is normally undertaken by individual experts or institutions which need the terms, usually following the free term translation method which, as has been shown above, is itself time-consuming. The terms thus prepared are then submitted to the NSC for further discussion, standardisation and formal approval. The process of 'standardising' and formally approving the terms includes so many phases and involves so many different groups of people (*viz.* the subject experts who initially coin the terms, the staff at the NSC's Standardisation Department, Members of Regional Swahili Committees, delegates of the NSC's Standardisation Committee and, finally, all members of the NSC) that it is cumbersome and unnecessarily long. (See Dunn, 1985, and Mwansoko, in preparation, for a detailed discussion of Swahili terminology standardisation procedures.) For example, although the IKR Literature Section's draft list of the literature terms was completed by 1979, it was formally approved by the NSC only in 1984, i.e. after a period of five years.

The efforts to disseminate the approved terminology lists have yielded very few practical results owing to the unclear demarcation of responsibilities among the institutions involved in the promotion and development of Swahili language. Officially the dissemination of Swahili technical terms is the responsibility of the NSC (see *Kakulu* No. 3, 1982: 6). After the terms have been approved as standard, they are listed in handouts, which are eventually published as *Tafsiri Sanifu* (Standard Translations) booklets and distributed to the Principal Secretaries of the various ministries, all Swahili promoting institutions in the country (for example, IKR, the Institute of Curriculum Development, the Swahili Department of the University of Dar es Salaam, the Institute of Swahili and Foreign Languages — Zanzibar, etc.) and the Regional and District Cultural Officers. It is anticipated by the NSC that those who received its terminology lists would reproduce and distribute them to the prospective register users in their ministries, educational institutions, regions and districts. At the NSC itself there is a large collection of terminology lists which can be given (upon request) to any visitor or can be sent, on request, to interested register users. However, investigations made by this author (Mwansoko, in preparation) have shown that, although the NSC expects the other language-related institutions to reproduce the standardised terms they receive from the NSC and distribute them to their respective register users, these institutions understand that officially this is not their responsibility but that of the NSC. They are therefore reluctant to do so.

This seemingly unco-operative relationship between the NSC and the other Swahili promoting institutions might have its roots in the parliamentary act which established the NSC in 1967. The act, among other things, requires the NSC to co-operate with the other Swahili promoting bodies in elaborating Swahili technical terms and to co-ordinate their terminology work. It does not, however, state how the NSC would co-operate with them and how it would co-ordinate their terminological activities. As a result, most of the NSC's terminology activities are a repetition of what is being undertaken by the other bodies; hence there is mistrust and competition between the NSC and these bodies instead of genuine co-operation (cf. Haule, 1983: 29–30). Moreover, although the NSC expects interested register users to contact it to obtain the necessary terminology lists, my research findings (Mwansoko, in preparation) indicate that the Council has not widely publicised itself to most of the prospective register users, including school and college students. Hence only a tiny proportion of the potential Swahili terminology users know of the NSC's terminology work.

These are but a few examples of practical problems pertaining to current terminology work in Swahili. They are serious problems which require concerted efforts to solve them. I challenge my colleagues (i.e. Swahili terminologists) to devote their energy and expertise to solving the above terminology-related problems instead of being frustrated as a result of the new post-primary education medium policy. We should strive to reduce the time factor in the code elaboration process, and to raise the quantity and quality of the Swahili terminologies as well as their chances of acceptability by their prospective users.

A Strategy of Future Terminology Work

There is even more work for Swahili terminologists in the immediate future. All terminology practitioners know that 'any process of word-coining in a specialised field should start first from the recording of existing terms concerning the given field' (Ohly & Gibbe, 1982: 37). This means that the first major task facing terminologists is to collect and record the existing Swahili terms in various subject fields. This work is now being done by the Terminology and Translation Section of the IKR; terms on agriculture and motor vehicle industry are currently being collected by the Section's researchers. But perhaps the most difficult work will be the systematisation of the existing terms as well as the ones being collected. As has been indicated earlier in this chapter, all of the existing Swahili terminology lists and index cards are arranged in alphabetical order — a practice which is against the requirements of modern terminology work (Johnson & Sager, 1980). According to modern terminology theory developed by the International Organisation for Standardisation (ISO) the basis of any term is the concept underlying it. Any systematic approach to terminology development should start with the analysis and systematisation of the technical concepts according to specialised subject fields. It is only after identifying the systems of concepts that terms can be assigned to them. The conceptual approach to terminological modernisation is advantageous in that it enables related concepts and terms to be grouped together, facilitates the elucidation of their meanings and brings about a fuller coverage of the subject fields (Picht & Draskan, 1985; Felber, 1980). Preparatory work to systematise the Swahili technical terms has also begun at the Terminology and Translation Section of the IKR. It should be noted that both terminology collection and systematisation are continuous undertakings and, hence, no one should be deceived into thinking that this work will be finished, either tomorrow or in the next decade.

The second task requiring the attention of terminologists is the preparation of comprehensive and detailed guidelines of Swahili terminology modernisation and their dissemination (through seminars or workshops or handouts) to the various subject experts who are interested in coining terminologies for their respective professions. Such experts may include school, college and university teachers, agricultural and veterinary officers, medical doctors, technicians and engineers, etc. The idea here is to ensure that specialised technical terms are prepared by the subject specialists themselves in order to guarantee their quality and acceptability. As Ferguson (1968: 33) has noted, 'lexical expansion . . . seems to take place most effectively when . . . the practitioners who need the vocabulary are involved in its creation'. And this is the procedure of terminology work recommended by the ISO and being followed by many national and international language modernisation agencies (see examples of such agencies in the *International Journal of the Sociology of Language* 23, 1980). The principles of Swahili terminological modernisation should be prepared by the NSC in conjunction with the IKR's Terminology and Translation Section. Elaboration of technical terms following clear guidelines will produce terms which are efficient and consistent.

Thirdly, efforts should be made to devise a more effective strategy of disseminating the Swahili terminologies which have been or are being developed, for without this the work of the terminologists will, of necessity, go to waste. Thus the issue of distributing language planning products among the prospective users is very important and can never be overstated. Jernudd & Das Gupta (1971: 206) have rightly claimed that 'the most important function in any prospective language-planning effort is to judge the spread-alternatives for suggested linguistic solutions'.

The dissemination of the Swahili terminologies is officially being done by the NSC, but as we have shown above, this exercise has yielded very few practical results. It is not easy to suggest an effective solution to this problem in this short discussion, as some empirical studies to test various alternative channels of promulgation will be necessary before one makes any concrete suggestions. Nevertheless, I am convinced that if individuals and professional groups who create the Swahili terms they need were allowed to disseminate them directly to their colleagues, perhaps there would be a solution to this problem (cf. Jernudd & Das Gupta, 1971: 210). Such experts or groups of experts know exactly who their colleagues are, where they are, and which terminologies they need. The only caution to be considered here is that the terms elaborated by these experts should follow the general principles of terminological modernisation laid down by the official institution(s) co-ordinating terminology work in general and be formally approved by these institutions. In addition, copies of the terms so formed should be retained by the co-ordinating institution(s) which will then record and store them on index cards or, if the facilities are available, in the computer for further references by other interested register users.

Conclusion

Our major concern in this chapter was to discuss the role of Swahili terminologists in the implementation of the present language policy in Tanzania. We have shown through this discussion that, although the current language policy might overtly seem to discourage further terminological modernisation in Swahili, especially for educational purposes, in reality there is still a lot of work to be done by Swahili terminologists. There are a number of serious terminological problems, theoretical as well as methodological, which require practical solutions by terminology experts. A challenge has been given to all those involved in Swahili terminology development to ensure that not only are the problems pertaining to the existing terminologies alleviated, but that more efficient Swahili terms are elaborated following 'scientifically' laid down principles.

References

ABDULAZIZ, M.H. 1972, Tanzania national language policy and the rise of Swahili political culture. In L. CLIFFE and J.S. SAUL (eds) *Socialism in Tanzania: An Interdisciplinary Reader*, Vol. I. Nairobi: East African Publishing House, pp. 155–64.
— 1980, The ecology of Tanzanian national language policy. In E.C.POLOMÉ and C.P. HILL (eds) *Language in Tanzania*. London: International Africa Institute/OUP, pp. 139–75.
DUNN, A.S. 1985, Swahili policy implementation in Tanzania: The role of the National Swahili Council (BAKITA), *Studies in the Linguistic Sciences* 15, 1 (Spring), 31–47.
FELBER, H. 1980, International standardisation of terminology: Theoretical and methodological aspects, *International Journal of the Sociology of Language* 23, 65–79.
FERGUSON, C. 1968, Language development. In J.A. FISHMAN *et al.* (eds), *Language Problems of Developing Nations*. New York: Wiley, pp. 27–36.
FISHMAN, J.A. 1977, Comparative study of language planning: Introducing a survey. In J. RUBIN *et al.* (eds) *Language Planning Processes*. The Hague: Mouton, pp. 31–9.
GIBBE, A.G. 1981, Istilahi za Fonolojia: Tatizo katika Usanifishaji wa Lugha ya Kiswahili. Paper presented at the Second Seminar of the Phonological Association of Tanzania, Dar es Salaam, December 1981.
HAULE, R.J.M. 1983, Hali na Matatizo ya Uandishi wa Vitabu vya Kiada. In TUKI, *Makala za Semina ya Kimataifa ya Waandishi wa Kiswahili II: Uandishi na Uchapishaji*, Dar es Salaam, pp. 18–31.

HILL, C.P. 1980, Some developments in language and education in Tanzania since 1969. In E.C. POLOMÉ and C.P. HILL (eds) *Language in Tanzania*. London: International Africa Institute, pp. 362–404.

JERNUDD, B. and DAS GUPTA, J. 1971, Towards a theory of language planning. In J. RUBIN and B. JERNUDD (eds) *Can Language Be Planned?* Honolulu: University of Hawaii Press.

JOHNSON, R.L. and SAGER, J.C. 1980, Standardisation of terminology in a model of Communication. *International Journal of the Sociology of Language* 23, 81–104.

kakulu (1982) No. 3, Kamati ya Kusanifu Lugha, BAKITA.

KHAMISI, A.M. 1980, Language Planning Processes in Tanzania. Paper presented at the Summer Institute on Language Planning with Respect to Minority Languages and Tribes, Central Institute of Indian Languages, Mysore, India, June/July 1980.

— 1986, Current Trends in Language Standardisation in Tanzania. Paper presented at the International Symposium on Language Standardisation in Africa, Mainz, W. Germany, 10–14 March 1986.

MACWILLIAM, A. 1985, Some thoughts on translation of scientific terminology in Kiswahili. *Kiswahili* 52/1 and 52/2, 114–28.

— 1986, Mbinu za Kupata Istilahi Kutokana na Lugha za Kibantu. Paper presented at BAKITA's Workshop on Language Standardisation Strategies, Dar es Salaam, 5–7 May 1986.

MDEE, J.S. 1983, The policy of adopting loan words in Kiswahili as conceived by BAKITA: a critique. *Multilingua* 2/2.

MORRISON, D.R. 1976, *Education and Politics in Africa: The Tanzanian Case*. London: Hurst.

MWANSOKO, H.J.M. (in preparation), *The Modernisation of Swahili Technical Terminologies: An Investigation of the Linguistics and Literature Terminologies*. DPhil Thesis, University of York.

NSC 1984, *Istilahi za Fasihi* (mimeo).

OHLY, R. and GIBBE, A.G. 1982, Language development: Lexical elaboration of Kiswahili to meet new educational demands. In H.R. TRAPPES-LOMAX *et al.* (eds) *Changing Language Media*. University of Dar es Salaam, pp. 36–43.

PICHT, H. and DRASKAN, J. 1985, *Terminology: An Introduction*. University of Surrey, Department of Linguistics and International Studies.

POLOMÉ, E.C. 1980, Tanzanian Language Policy and Swahili. *Word* 30.

RUBAGUMYA, C.M. 1986, Language planning in the Tanzanian educational system: Problems and prospects. *Journal of Multilingual and Multicultural Development* 7, 4, 283–300.

SELANDER, E. 1980, Language for professional use from the Swedish point of view. *International Journal of the Sociology of Language* 23, 17–28.

TEMU, C.W. 1986, *Towards the Adoption of Kiswahili as a Working Language of the Organisation of African Unity and Regional Institutions in East and Central Africa*. Technical Report for the OAU/UNESCO (mimeo).

TRAPPES-LOMAX, H.R., BESHA, R.M. and MCHA, Y.Y. (eds) 1982, *Changing Language Media*. Papers from the Seminar 'The Impact on the University of the Expected Change in the Medium of Instruction in the Secondary Schools', University of Dar es Salaam.

TUMBO, Z. 1982, Towards a systematic terminology development in Kiswahili. *Kiswahili* 49/1, 87–93.

13 Political and economic dimensions to language policy options in Tanzania

C.M. RUBAGUMYA and A.F. LWAITAMA

Introduction

In this chapter, we discuss the problems underlying the current language policy in Tanzania and suggest alternative options that may assist in the resolution of those problems. Our point of departure is that language policy has to be placed within the framework of a wider political and economic context of society. We argue that, given the current level of socio-economic underdevelopment of Tanzania, the present policy can only retard, rather than accelerate, our development. It is important to stress this point because the proponents of the present language policy give as their main argument the need for Tanzania to 'catch up' with the rest of the world in scientific and technological development. For example, in 1983 the Minister for Education said: 'We must learn from foreign nations and in order to do so we must use English to promote understanding [of what is learnt] in schools' (quoted in Schmied, 1986: 109).

The Current Policy

Very briefly stated, the current language policy in education consists of:

— teaching Kiswahili as a subject to all pupils at primary and secondary school level,
— teaching all subjects (except English) in Kiswahili at primary school level,
— teaching siasa (political education) in Kiswahili at secondary school level,

143

— teaching all the other subjects in English at secondary and tertiary levels of education.

Several assumptions underlie the present policy. First, it is assumed that it is possible to teach in English at all levels where English is currently the medium of instruction. In other words, students are assumed to be adequately proficient in English to be taught in that language. This assumption is questioned by several chapters in this volume, especially that by Trappes-Lomax.

Secondly, it is assumed that all (or at least most) teachers and instructors called upon to teach in English have adequate levels of fluency to enable them to do so as envisaged, and that this position has not changed over the years and is not expected to change in the near future.

Thirdly, for the proponents of the present policy, the most cost-effective means of gaining access to scientific and technological advances in the world as a whole (e.g. through documentation, conferences and exchange of personnel) is to have *as many Tanzanians as possible* acquire adequate levels of fluency in English for that purpose. The alternative option of training *a few* Tanzanians to gain access to such knowledge in English and then having these Tanzanians make such knowledge available to *as many Tanzanians as possible in Kiswahili* is rejected.

Fourthly, it is assumed that adequate levels of fluency in English for the purposes of gaining access to scientific and technological advances in the world as a whole cannot be achieved if English is not used as the medium of instruction. However, people in other parts of the world master foreign languages without having to use them as media of instruction.

Finally, it is assumed that all knowledge currently being generated in the world is originally in English, and that all foreign personnel currently working in Tanzania are competent in English.

Problems inherent in current policy options

The main problems inherent in this policy can be summarised as follows:

a. It is difficult to envisage a situation where there will be sufficient numbers of teachers and other instructors with adequate levels of fluency in English to implement the present policy option (see next section).

b. Where local publishing in English is difficult, foreign currency would be required for the importation of books and other teaching materials, and this dependency on foreign resources may prove unsustainable. This problem is currently, perhaps, made less obvious by the British Government-funded English Language Support Project.

c. It is further difficult to envisage a situation whereby the currently acknowledged inadequacies among students in the mastering of the English language as a medium of instruction would be eliminated in the foreseeable future. This being the case, difficulties may be encountered in fulfilling the country's manpower training targets. (Yahya-Othman in this volume discusses some of the implications of this aspect of the current policy options.)

d. It can be assumed that communication problems must be experienced where foreign technical assistance personnel with inadequate levels of fluency in English work with their Tanzanian counterparts whose level of English fluency is equally inadequate. Technological transfer is in this case likely to be hampered, thus adversely affecting Tanzania's socio-economic development.

Alternative Policy Options

The alternative options are based on the following assumptions relating to the current problems.

Firstly, relating to the problem of the shortage of teachers and instructors with the requisite knowledge of English, we assume that this problem is likely to be exacerbated by the *political* impossibility of stemming the tide of the proliferation of secondary and tertiary level institutions. Political education in Tanzania since 1967 appears to have made it difficult for significant regional–ethnic imbalances in educational provision to be easily accepted. Unless this 'mushrooming' of secondary and tertiary institutions is matched by appropriate teacher training, which is not the case at the moment, the problem of teachers who are not proficient in English will remain.

Secondly, with respect to the problem of dependency on foreign funding for securing books and other educational materials, we assume that it is impossible to continue receiving such foreign funding as would be adequate to meet the ever-increasing demand for secondary and tertiary education. Even if it were possible one could argue that it is undesirable both economically and politically. Economically, such dependency would tend to stifle the development of indigenous scientific and technological capacities with respect to local publishing of educational materials. This would in turn tend to accentuate Tanzania's economic dependency, thus further weakening its political sovereignty. Tanzania's non-aligned posture in international relations which, since 1964, has facilitated diversification in the sources of foreign funding for its development programmes could then be put in jeopardy. The international economic situation in the 1980s does not augur well for availability of foreign funds for socio-economic development in countries like Tanzania. This should be all the more reason for diversification of the possible sources of such funding. One could further argue that such a hostile international economic climate demands that even diversification in foreign sources of funding for socio-economic development is not the basic solution to these countries' problems. The situation would seem to demand the development of indigenous scientific and technological capacities on a self-reliant basis. We assume that these countries will eventually realise this and act accordingly.

Thirdly, as far as the problem of the student's mastery of English as the medium of education is concerned, we assume that the sociolinguistic environment prevailing in Tanzania today will inevitably lead to Kiswahili taking over (initially in a *de facto* manner) as the medium of education. It appears to us that policy makers will eventually have to address themselves to this inevitability of Kiswahili becoming the medium of instruction. It is not helpful to sit back and pretend that this inevitability could be reversed, especially given the inadequacies in foreign funding currently available for the financing of projects to boost the teaching of English in secondary and tertiary education. We think that it is better to start planning now for the inevitable change of media rather than leave such change to occur in a spontaneous and haphazard manner. We suspect that the country's entire educational system is likely to be damaged substantially if current trends are allowed to continue unchecked. (Also see Yahya-Othman in this volume.)

Fourthly, in relation to possible communication difficulties between foreign and local technicians working on foreign-funded development projects, we assume that there are more foreign technicians from non-English-speaking countries than there are from English-speaking ones.

A general survey of foreign countries that have supported Tanzania's major development programmes in the 1980s bears out our assumption (Baregu, 1988). There has been a substantial contribution made by the Nordic countries, the Netherlands and the Federal Republic of Germany to water provision programmes in the country, for example (see Table 13.1).

The Ministry of Water's Master Planning Co-ordination Unit was established with Nordic assistance in 1980.

In the agricultural sector, the Netherlands has provided Tanzania with more technical personnel assistance than any other single foreign source in the period 1970/71 to 1986/87 (Msambichaka & Rugumyamheto, 1987). There have also been substantial contributions made by Japan in the field of power rehabilitation and road construction (*Daily News* – *Tanzania*, 5.3.1988). Other countries such as The People's Republic of China, The Democratic People's Republic of Korea, and the Islamic Republic of Iran have also made significant contributions with technical assistance personnel, especially in the field of modern farming involving irrigation (*Daily News*, 7.2.1988). The Soviet Union and the German Democratic Republic have also committed many resources involving technical assistance personnel in technical education, in addition to involvement in other fields.

We assume that processes of technological transfer in Tanzania would be enhanced if there were no assumption on the part of foreign technicians that Tanzania was an English-speaking country! Until Kiswahili becomes both the *de facto* and the *de jure* medium of education at secondary and tertiary levels of education this erroneous tendency to anglicise Tanzania will persist, with the consequences which it entails in respect to the potential for communication difficulties between foreign and local technical personnel on foreign-funded projects.

Below are the alternative policy options which could be implemented in the order in which they occur.

First, counterpose the current policy option of teaching in English in all secondary schools with a policy of teaching in English in only a *few* secondary schools. Let admission to these admittedly élite schools be competitive on the basis of student ability rather than parental economic strength or social status. Switch the medium of education in the rest of the secondary schools to Kiswahili in a planned manner. We consider all claims that such a policy option will be élitist to be demagogic, as the current policy option is equally élitist with the difference that it is élitism based on parental economic and/or social status rather than students' ability.

A non-élitist policy will be one where every primary school leaver has the opportunity of entering secondary school and where the sociolinguistic environment is equally favourable to all students wishing to acquire adequate levels of fluency in English. The current policy option penalises students whose parents' economic and social status does not facilitate such students' acquisition of English. In the alternative policy option we are proposing, students such as these are given a *real* choice between pursuing secondary education in English or in Kiswahili.

TABLE 13.1 *Donors in the Tanzania water programme*

Region	Water project	Donor
1. Kagera	Rural water supply	Swedish International Development Agency
	Bukoba urban water supply	Italian Government
2. Mara	Rural water supply	Swedish International Development Agency
	Musoma urban water supply	Italian Government
3. Mwanza	Rural water supply	Swedish International Development Agency
	Urban water supply	European Economic Community (EEC)
4. Shinyanga	Rural water supply	Dutch Government
	Urban water supply	African Development Bank
5. Singida	Rural water supply	Australian Government (have left the country); Tanzania Christian Refugee Service
	Manyoni District	Precious Blood Fathers
6. Dodoma	Rehabilitation of rural water supply	Water Aid (British Government)
	Mwisanga/Ntomoko Project	Christian Council of Tanzania (CCT)
7. Morogoro	Rural water supply	Dutch Government
8. Mtwara	Rural water supply	Finnish International Development Agency (FINNIDA)
	Urban water supply	European Economic Community (EEC)
9. Coast	Bagamoyo rural water supply	Danish International Development Agency (DANIDA)
10. Lindi	Rural water supply	Finnish International Development Agency (FINNIDA)
11. Mbeya	Rural water supply	Finnish International Development Agency (FINNIDA)
	Urban water supply	European Economic Community (EEC)

TABLE 13.1 *Continued*

Region	Water project	Donor
12. Ruvuma	Rural water supply	Danish International Development Agency (DANIDA)
13. Iringa	Rural water supply	Danish International Development Agency (DANIDA)
14. Kigoma	Rural water supply	Norwegian Agency for International Development (NORAD)
15. Arusha	Urban water supply	Government of the Federal Republic of Germany
16. Tanga	Rural water supply	Government of the Federal Republic of Germany
	Urban water supply	Government of the Federal Republic of Germany
17. Rukwa	Rural water supply	Norwegian Agency for International Development (NORAD)
18. Kilimanjaro	Water master plan	Japanese Government
19. Tabora	Water master plan	World Bank
20. D'Salaam	Water master plan	Canadian International Development Agency (CIDA)

Source: Daily News — Tanzania, 22.3.88.

Second, continue with the current policy of teaching English as a subject in all secondary schools and improve on the implementation of this by setting realistic objectives to guide ELT. Also explore possibilities of student exchange programmes with countries where English is predominantly used, e.g. Australia, New Zealand, Canada, USA, Jamaica.

Third, discontinue the present policy of teaching English as a subject at primary school level. Instead, strengthen implementation of the current policy of teaching Kiswahili as a subject and the teaching of all other subjects in Kiswahili. (The gradual shift in the status of English from being a second language to being a foreign one would seem to justify its removal from the primary school curriculum.)

Fourth, from both the Kiswahili-medium and the English-medium secondary schools select a number of schools where other foreign languages will be offered as optional subjects. These foreign languages do not have to be only West European. If current patterns of international co-operation continue (with Tanzania increasingly co-operating more with non-English-speaking countries than with English-speaking ones), then languages such as Japanese, Korean, Arabic, Swedish, Norwegian, Dutch, German, Russian, Chinese, Spanish, French, Danish and Finnish could be selected. It is not being suggested that all these languages be offered as options in any one school. Nor is it being suggested that they be offered immediately and all at the same time and at the same level.

Fifth, Kiswahili should eventually be the main medium of education at tertiary level. Only in a few élite institutes of foreign languages would the relevant foreign languages be used as media. In all tertiary institutions English is likely to remain the most important foreign language for most students to have a functional knowledge of; therefore, English for Specific Purposes (ESP) programmes should be established in all tertiary institutions. However, the ESP programmes currently organised by quite a number of Communication Skills (in English) Units may need to be re-examined in the light of all the elements constituting the proposed alternative policy options.

Sixth, programmes in the teaching of a number of foreign languages (other than English) for specific purposes should also, where possible, be established. A French language programme offered in the Faculty of Engineering at the University of Dar es Salaam for a number of years demonstrates that this policy option is not far fetched. There is no reason why, for example, a course in Japanese for Specific Purposes (JSP) should not be offered to finalist students in the Department of Electrical Engineering, nor is there any reason why a course in Arabic for Specific Purposes (ASP) should not be offered to students undertaking specialist studies in Kiswahili, whose modern lexicon is said to have borrowed several lexical items from Arabic (Kihore, 1983: 164).

Conclusion

We have discussed policy options which appear to have been taken by the current political leadership in Tanzania. As in most African countries, the main option has been to continue with the use of the language of the former colonial power in as many fields of communication as possible. Unlike the position in many other African countries, however, Tanzania opted quite early to intensify and extend the use of an indigenous language,

Kiswahili, as the language of wider communication in the political and social spheres. The adoption of this language policy option, bolstered by some of the political and economic measures taken to implement the Arusha Declaration on the building of 'a socialist and self-reliant country', would appear to have set in motion processes leading to the present situation whereby English has virtually ceased to be a viable medium of communication in the education system as a whole (Criper & Dodd, 1984; Trappes-Lomax, this volume).

We have looked at the problems inherent in the options that have been taken, suggesting that the assumptions on which the options were based were erroneous. We have put forward alternative policy options based on assumptions which are, in our view, more plausible.

Tanzania would appear to be facing a crisis in language policy formulation which some observers may find hard to understand. On the one hand, it is often cited as an example of a country in sub-Saharan Africa which is an exception (together with Somalia and Ethiopia) to the rule that 'foreign colonial languages are more favoured now than they were before independence' (Mateene, quoted by Phillipson et al., 1986: 91). Tanzania is seen as a country which has opted to promote the widest possible use of an indigenous language. On the other hand, it has, especially since 1983, opted to rationalise (like every other sub-Saharan African country) the continued use of a 'colonial language' as a medium of education at the secondary and tertiary levels.

The political and economic dimensions of the current and the proposed alternative policy options are not hard to see. The current policy options are based on the assumption that African countries cannot develop socially and economically without the assistance of former European colonial powers; hence the perceived necessity to continue to rely on the use of languages of former European colonial powers for wider communication in the sphere of scientific and technological education.

The alternative policy options that we propose are based on the assumption that African countries are actually unlikely to develop if they continue to rely to a large extent on technical assistance from former European colonial powers. Current political and economic trends in the world dictate a reappraisal of past language policy options which did not give due weight to the need for *diversification* in international contacts and the *intensification* of efforts to develop indigenous capacities. Political and economic necessity would seem to dictate that African countries begin teaching some of their people Japanese, German, Russian, Korean, Chinese, etc. through the medium of African languages rather than through the medium of English, French or Portuguese. These trends will also tend to

demand that African countries must begin to disseminate both elementary
and advanced technical information in languages in which most of their
peoples are most fluent. As the Kenyan writer Ngugi wa Thiongo (1986: 26)
has put it, even 'the most zealous of European missionaries who believed in
rescuing Africa from itself, even from the paganism of its languages, were
nevertheless masters of African languages which they often reduced to
writing'. Contemporary political and economic leaders in Africa are likely
to be forced by current political and economic necessity to begin to learn
from the European Christian missionaries *vis-à-vis* the use of indigenous
African languages.

References

BAREGU, M. 1988, The Arusha declaration paradox, or how a self-reliance policy
    reinforced Tanzania's dependence. *Maji Maji,* No. 46.
CRIPER, C. and DODD, W.A. 1984, *Report on the Teaching of English Language
    and its use as a Medium in Education in Tanzania.* Dar es Salaam: The British
    Council.
KIHORE, Y.M. 1983, Maandishi ya Kiarabu yaliyo na umuhimu kwa Kiswahili.
    Makala za Semina ya Kimataifa ya Waandishi wa Kiswahili. Institute of
    Kiswahili Research, Dar es Salaam.
MSAMBICHAKA, L.A. and RUGUMYAMHETO, J.A. 1987, *A Study of High Level
    Agricultural Manpower and Technical Assistance.* Draft report submitted to
    the Tanzanian Ministry of Agriculture/FAO, Dar es Salaam.
NGUGI WA THIONGO 1986, *Decolonizing the Mind: The Politics of Language in
    African Literature.* London: James Currey.
PHILLIPSON, R. *et al.* 1986, Namibian educational language planning: English for
    liberation or neo-colonialism? In B. SPOLSKY (ed.) *Language and Education in
    Multilingual Settings.* Clevedon: Multilingual Matters.
SCHMIED, J.J. 1986, English in Tanzanian education. *Bayreuth African Studies
    Series* No. 5.

Index

Note: Page references in *italics* indicate tables and figures.

Abdulaziz-Mkilifi, M.H. 10
Acquisition, natural 96, 97
Africanisation, of English *125*, 125, 126
Afrikaans 46
Arabic, as second language 20, 150
Arusha Declaration 17, 98, 151
Attitudes 95, 131
  –to English 29-30, 48, 60-1, 63, 78, 84-5
  –to Kiswahili 48
Authenticity 3, 94, 96, 101, 111

BAKITA (National Swahili Council) 50, 98, 136-8, 140
Ban, language 22n., 27, 30
Bantu languages 8, *127*, 128, 136
Batibo, H.M. 36, 54-74
Behaviour, language 123, 125-9, 131
Bhaji, A.F. 76
Bilingualism 9, 25, 32, 34, 42, 51-2
Binns Mission Report 7-8, 17
Book Development Council of Tanzania (BAVITA) 64
Books, *see* materials, teaching; reference books; textbooks
Botswana, national language 75
Britain,
  –colonial rule 7-9, 16-17
  –Overseas Development Administration 27, 99
British Council 37-8
Broughton, M. 38
Brumfit, C.J. & Roberts, J.T. 96
Bull, W.E. 94-5
Burt, M. & Dulay, H. 96
Burundi,
  –and Kiswahili 5, 10
  –national language 75

Cameron, J. & Dodd, W. 8
Canada, bilingualism 51
Chama Cha Mapinduzi 134
Chichewa, as second language 20
Choice, language 75
Chonjo, P.N. 17
Christianity, and language in education 6-7
Chwa, Sir Daudi 6, 7
Class size 63
Code-switching 12, 32-3, 76
Cognition, and language 49, 50-1, 68, 97
Colonisation,
  –and language policies 7-8, 15-18, 123
  –and language spread 5-6
Communication skills 110-12, 114-15, 118-21
Communication Skills Unit 49, 105-16
  –evaluation 115-16
  –and language problem 106-9, 114
  –remedial courses 109-15
Competence,
  –descriptive 79, 86
  –linguistic 2, 79, 89-90, 100, 106-7
  –pedagogic 65-6, 89-90, 100
  –productive/communicative 44, 50, 89-92, 106-7
  –receptive 44
  –target 20, 21n.
Conceptualisation 50-1, 57, 95
Conflict, language 43-52
Conversion courses 40

Corder, S.P. 112
Criper, C. & Dodd, W.A. 26-7, 28-9,
  36-41, 43, 49, 52, 99-102, 108
Criper, C. & Widdowson, H.G. 94

Dar es Salaam University,
  Communication Skills Unit 49,
  105-16
Dede Kamkondo, W.C. 108-9
Denny, N. 105
Dependency, economic 146
Development, and language 2, 18, 20,
  31, 43-8, 51, 143, 145-6, 151
Developmentalism 19, 21
Discourse analysis 34
Domains, language 10-13, *11*, 29,
  47-50, 76-7
Dunn, A.S. 21n., 136

Education,
  –adult 34-5
  –and development 43, 45-6
  –higher 18, 45
  –planning 15
  –primary 34, 55-6
  –private 26, 58
  –secondary 18, 34
  –for Self-Reliance 2-3, 34, 98
Education and language 1-3, 94-7,
  100-3, 115-16, 134-5, 139, 143-4,
  151
  –primary 1, 7, 20, 54-74
    English 45
    Kiswahili 26, 30, 32, 36, 44, 46-7,
      67, 76, 85, 99, 133, 143, 149
  –secondary 2, 7, 21n., 45-9, 101
    English 26-8, 31-2, 36-41, 44,
      47-9, 68-9, 72, 76-7, 98, 102,
      144, 147
    Kiswahili 28-32, 35, 36-8, 49, 67,
      70-2, 76, 101, 134, 143-4, 147
  –tertiary 10, 13, 21n., 34-5
    English 36, 38, 48-9, 77, 98, 102,
      105-16, 144
    Kiswahili 1-2, 35, 41, 49, 134, 150
Élitism, in education 2, 34, 72, 147
Ellis, Rod 39
ELT,
  –as differentiated 16-17, 18-19, 20,
    21n.
  –as endogenous 16-17, 18, 19-20,
    21n.
  –as exogenous 16, 17-18, 21, 39-40
  –history 15-21, 38
  –language of instruction 20, 85-6,
    149
  –in primary schools 54-74, 78
  –status 56-64
  –transition phase 17-18
  –as undifferentiated 16, 17-18, 21
English,
  –and development 2
  –East African 123-32
  –Educated East African 123, 131
  –as foreign language 29, 47, 98-100,
    102-3, 129, 149-50
  –functions 76-8
  –as international language 13, 20,
    27, 123-4, 129-31
  –as library language 13, 41
  –as official language 12-13, 75
  –as second language 30, 102-3, 124,
    129-31, 149
  –for Specific Purposes (ESP) 150
  –Standard 126, 128-9, 131
  –Standard African 129
  –standards 28-9, 48, 49, 52, 54, 56,
    74, 78, 99-103, 107-8, 125
  –status 26, 29, 48, 62-3, 90, 98-9,
    102
  –teaching, *see* ELT
  see also education and language;
    grammar; status, language
English Language Support Project 26,
  27, 29-30, 36-41, 145
  –background 36-8
  –evaluation 40-1
English, as medium of instruction 1-3,
  10, 51-2
  –history 7-8, 15-21
English for Tanzanian Schools 57
Environment,
  –natural language 95-6
  –sociolinguistic 27, 29, 34, 82, 85,
    89, 91-2, 102, 115, 123-4,
    134-5, 146-7
ESL, *see* English, as L2
Exposure,
  –to English 62-3, 66-7, 68, 80, 82-6,
    91-2, 100, 102-3

–to Kiswahili 8-9
Ezekiel, J.R. 57, 59

Fasold, R. 1-2
Ferguson, C. 140
Fisher, J.C. 112-13
Fishman, J.A. 133
FLT 15, 16, 18-19, 21n.
Fossilisation, language 112
French,
 –as foreign language 150
 –as medium of instruction 2, 3, 44
 –as second language 20

German, as medium of instruction 6,
 16
Germany, colonial rule 5-6
Ghana, language of instruction 2
Grammar,
 –English 107-10, 128-9, *130*
 –Kiswahili 7
Gregorios, M.P. 19

Hausa, as L2 20
Hymes, D. 106-7

Immersion programmes 44, 102
Institute of Kiswahili Research (IKR)
 33, 135-6, 137, 139-40
Intensive Grammar Programme
 (IGP) 107, 109-10, 116, 117-18
Inter-territorial Language Committee
 50
Interlanguages 125, 131
International Organisation for
 Standardisation (ISO) 139-40
Isayev, M.I. 19
Islam, and use of Kiswahili 6, 10

Jarvis, J. 57, 58-9
Jernudd, B. & Das Gupta, J. 140
Johnson, K. 107
Judiciary, language use *11*, *12*, 12-13,
 133

Kachru, B.B. 89-90
Kapinga, M.K. 15-22, 25-35
Katigula, B.A.J. 58, 59
Kavugha, D. & Bobb, D. 12
KELT staff 39, 40, 65

Kenya,
 –and English 98, 123-4, 126-31, *127*
 –and Kiswahili 5, 6, 7, 10
Kiswahili,
 –and development 2, 18, 20, 31,
  43-4
 –history 5-9
 –as international language 42-3, 48
 –as language of administration 6, 8,
  10, 76-7, 98, 133, 134
 –linguistic development 7, 30, 50,
  133-41
 –as national language 1, 9, 46, 48,
  75-6, 85, 99, 123, 133
 –as official language 133
 –as second language 8-9, 94
 –standards 52
 –use punished 22n.
 see also education and language;
  grammar; status, language;
  terminology
Kiswahili, as medium of instruction,
 –advantages 2-3, 25, 26, 27-32, 134-
  5, 146-7
 –disadvantages 1-2, 30-2
 –historical 6-8
 –opposition to 6-8
Kkrumah, Kwame 2
Knowledge, access to 2, 19, 37, 78,
 97, 144
Krashen, S.D. 96

Language,
 –foreign 96-7, 102-3, 149-50
 –international 13, 20, 27, 31, 42-3,
  51, 123
 –library 13, 41
 –national 1, 9, 43, 75, 85, 123, 133
 –official 12, 85, 96, 133
 –second 96
 –of wider communication 45, 46,
  96, 151
Le Page, R. 95
Learning Through Language' 69
Lesotho, national language 75
Lexis, East African 75-6, 125-6
Lingala, as second language 20
lingua franca, Kiswahili as 10, 16-17
Loan words 125, 136-7
Love, A. 117n.

Lwaitama, A.F. 15-22, 25-35, 36-41,
  143-52

Mcha, Y.Y. 116
Makweta, J. (Minister for Education)
  21n., 34, 37
Malawi, teaching of English 74, 116
Martin-Jones, Marilyn 25
Materials, teaching,
  –in English 39, 40, 48, 56-8, 61,
   64-5, 70, 72, 76, 84, 100, 116,
   145-6
  –in Kiswahili 30, 33, 34, 76
Mazrui, A.A. & Zirimu, P. 5, 6
Mbunda, F. *et al.* 101
Methods, teaching 33, 59, 61, 63, 69,
  116
  –communicative 124
  –extensive approach 68-9
  –intensive approach 69-70
  –maximalist approach 71
  –minimalist approach 71-2
  –and teacher training 80, 81-2, 84, 86
Mkude, D.J. 49
Mlahagwa, J.R. 17, 22n.
Mlama, P.O. & Matteru, M. 26, 43,
  49, 101-2
Modernisation, *see* terminology
Modernity 2, 94, 101
Mohamed, W.A. 98
Mohammed, M.A. 49
Moshi, E.A. 82-3
Mother tongue, in primary education
  44, 94, 95
Motivation,
  –to learn English 37, 55-6, 57, 60-2,
   63, 66, 70-2, 84-5, 113
  –to learn language 95
  –of teachers 58-60, 61, 70
Moumouni, A. 8-9
Mozambique, and Kiswahili 10
Multilingualism 45, 75-6
Muze, M.S. 66
Mwansoko, H.J.M. 133-41

Namibia, development 46
National Swahili Council (BAKITA)
  50, 98, 136-8, 140
Nationalism, and language planning
  1, 34, 136

Needs, language 15, 25, 31
Ngalasso, M.M. 2, 3
Ngugi wa Thiongo 152
Nyerere, Julius 21n., 31, 36-7

O'Barr, W.M. 9
Objectives, teaching 63-4, 67, 73
Ohly, R. & Gibbe, A.G. 139
Organisation of African Unity 135
Orthography, Kiswahili 7

Pearson, I. 38
Phillipson, R., Skutnabb-Kangas, T.
  & Africa, H. 1, 151
Planning, language,
  –colonial 17
  –modern 1, 20, 52, 94-103, 133-41
Policy, language 21n., 25-35, 78
  –alternative options 33-4, 68-72,
   145-50, 151
  –change in 36-7, 51-2, 67, 76-7
  –consequences 48-51, 88
  –and development 44, 52, 145
  –and education 1-3, 64, 67-8, 72-4,
   133-5, 139, 141, 143-5
  –recent developments 26-8
  –socio-economic context 17-18, 51,
   77, 143-52
Polomé, E. 67
Portuguese,
  –as medium of instruction 2
  –as second language 20
Presidential Commission on
  Education 36-7, 100-1
Primary English for Tanzania 65
Proficiency,
  –in English 27, 29, 37, 74, 78-92,
   99-100, 105, 115, 144
  –in Kiswahili 30
  –mother tongue 44
Pronunciation, of English 58, *125*,
  125, 126-8, *127*, 129
Punishment, and language use 22n.,
  27, 62-3

Rea, P. 106, 111-12, 114
Readers,
  –English 39, 40, 65, 67, 69
  –Kiswahili 33
Reading, in English 39-41, 57, 71, 102

Reference books 57-8, 64, 67, 71-2,
84
Roy-Campbell, Z.M. 75-93
Roy-Campbell, Z.M. & Qorro, M.P.
37
Rubagumya, C.M. 1-3, 5-13, 15-22,
25-35, 43, 143-52
Rugemalira, J.M. 25-35, 36-41, 43,
47, 105-21
Rwanda,
–and Kiswahili 5, 10
–national language 75

Schmied, J.J. 15, 27, 123-32, 143
Siasa (political education) 47, 49, 76,
143
Skills, language 70-1, 79, 90, 106,
109, 110-12, 124
Somalia,
–and Kiswahili 10
–national language 75
Sotho, as second language 20
Standardisation, language 7, 50, 95,
131-2, 137-8
Status, language 94-7, 98-9
–English 26, 29-30, 47-8, 62-3, 103,
129, 149
–Kiswahili 9, 30, 48, 133, 137
Strevens, P. 89
Study skills 110-11, 114, 115
Sudan, and Kiswahili 10
Swahili, see Kiswahili
Swaziland, national language 75
Switzerland, bilingualism 51
Syntax,
–East African English 126
–Kiswahili 7

TANU (Tanganyika African National
Union) 9
Teacher training 45, 65, 75-92, 116
–adequacy 82-3, 89-91, 145
–Degree course 81-2, 86-9
–Diploma course 79-80, 82, 83-6
–and English Literature 77, 82, 87-
8, 91
–in-service 65, 69, 79, 91, 92
Teachers,
–expatriate 31
–language use 30-1, 33, 35

–proficiency 144-5
language 49, 58, 65, 78-92
in teaching methods 58-60, 65-6,
89-90, 100
–shortage 87-8, 144, 145
–specialist 59, 69, 70-2
Technology transfer 145, 147
Terminology, modernisation 7, 30,
31, 33, 49-50, 75-6, 133-41
–evaluation 135-9
–future strategies 139-41
Tests, evaluation 71
Tetlow, J.G. 25-35
Textbooks 33, 34, 39, 50, 56-8, 59,
63-4, 66, 69, 71-2
–in English 76-7, 84-5, 91, 145
–ideology 40
Trappes-Lomax, H.R. 43, 47, 94-103,
144
Trappes-Lomax, H.R. & Besha,
R.M. 42
Trappes-Lomax, H.R., Besha, R.M.
& Mcha, Y.Y. 32
Trifocalism, linguistic 98, 123-4
Triglossia 10-12, *11*, 98
Tucker, Bishop 6, 17
Tume ya Rais ya Elimu 57, 58-9, 61,
63, 65-7, 73

Uganda,
–and English 74, 98
–and Kiswahili 5, 6, 7, 10
ujamaa 125
University Screening Test (UST) *107*,
107-8, 110, 112
University Teaching and Learning
Improvement Programme (UTLIP)
106
UPE (Universal Primary Education)
55, 57-60
Use, language 9-13, *11*, 76-7, 123-5,
124

Vernacular languages 7-8, 10, 12-13,
52, 76, 98, 123
–in education 45-6, 47
Vocabulary,
–English 39
–Kiswahili 30, 33, 49, 133-41
VSO staff 65

Wangwe, S.M. 17
Water provision programmes 146-7,
  148-9
Waters, A. 115
Weston, A.B. 99
Whiteley, W.H. 5, 6, 7, 98, 101

Yahya-Othman, S. 42-52, 134, 145

Zaire, language of instruction 2, 3,
  10
Zambia, and Kiswahili 10
Zanzibar, use of Kiswahili 7
Zimbabwe, teaching of English 74,
  116
Zulu, as second language 20